# Raw Outrage

Phil Mulloy is the punk bluesman of animation. His films are raw, minimalist, and ferociously satirical—short bursts of crude brilliance that confront the hypocrisies of religion, nationalism, masculinity, and class with uncompromising rage. If Disney represents the heart of animation, then Mulloy is its bowels—unafraid to reveal the grotesque underbelly of human nature.

With thick black lines, stick figures, and penis-nosed characters, Mulloy's deceptively primitive style delivers scathing critiques of modern society. He broke onto the scene in the 1990s with the blistering *Cowboys* series, followed by subversive classics like *The Sound of Music* and *The Ten Commandments.* In the 2000s, he pushed further with the sci-fi-influenced trilogy *Intolerance* and the deeply polarizing, yet groundbreaking, feature and short series *The Christies.*

This book traces Mulloy's singular career—his shocking early shorts, experimental features, and recent return with potent works like *Endgame* and *Once Upon a Time on Earth.* Part biography, part critical reflection, and part personal journey, *Raw Outrage* explores how Mulloy's work remains urgent in an age where animation often plays it safe.

Award-winning writer Chris Robinson guides readers through Mulloy's world with his usual passion, insight, and irreverent humor. What emerges is a portrait of an artist who refuses to be polite—whose films challenge, provoke, and endure.

**Chris Robinson** is a writer and the Artistic Director of the Ottawa International Animation Festival (OIAF). A prominent voice in the animation world, Robinson has been recognized with several prestigious honors, including the **Animafest Zagreb Award for Outstanding Contribution to Animation Studies** (2020) and the **Prix René Jodoin** (2022) for his contributions to Canadian animation. Described as "one of the most stylistically original and provocative experts in the history of animation," Robinson's influence spans writing, curation, and film.

He first gained attention through his eclectic and influential magazine column, *Animation Pimp*, which was later adapted into a book of the same name. His other animation books reflect a deep engagement with global animation, including *Unsung Heroes of Animation, Between Genius and Utter Illiteracy, Looking for A Place to Happen, Ballad of a Thin Man: In Search of Ryan Larkin*, *Animators Unearthed*, *Time Out of Mind*, *Earmarked for Collision*, *Cheer and Loathing in Animation*, and *Dreaming a way (of) Life*.

In addition to his work as a critic and historian, Robinson co-wrote the award-winning animated short *Lipsett Diaries* (2010), directed by Theodore Ushev. More recently, he collaborated with German artist Andreas Hykade on the illustrated novel *My Balls Are Killing Me*. He also wrote the script for Ushev's upcoming live-action feature film, *Idling*.

# Focus Animation

*Series Editor*

Chris Robinson is the Artistic Director of the Ottawa International Animation Festival (OIAF) and is a well-known figure in the animated film world. We welcome any submissions to help grow the wonderful content we are striving to provide to the animation community.

**The Focus Animation Series** aims to provide unique, accessible content that may not otherwise be published. We allow researchers, academics, and professionals the ability to quickly publish high impact, current literature in the field of animation for a global audience.

This series is a fine complement to the existing, robust animation titles available through CRC Press/Focal Press.

Nordic Animation Balancing the East and the West
*Liisa Vähäkylä*

Classic Chinese Animated Film and Ideology: Tradition, Innovation, and Interculturality
*Olga Bobrowska*

Cheer and Loathing: Scattered Ramblings on Indie Animation
*Chris Robinson*

Michel Ocelot: A World of Animated Images
*Laura Buono*

Dreaming a way (of) Life: The Films of Lewis Klahr
*Chris Robinson*

Raw Outrage: The Films of Phil Mulloy
*Chris Robinson*

For more information about this series, please visit: https://www.routledge.com/Focus-Animation/book-series/CRCFOCUSANI

# Raw Outrage
## The Films of Phil Mulloy

Chris Robinson

CRC Press
Taylor & Francis Group
Boca Raton London New York

CRC Press is an imprint of the
Taylor & Francis Group, an informa business

First edition published 2026
by CRC Press
2385 NW Executive Center Drive, Suite 320, Boca Raton FL 33431

and by CRC Press
4 Park Square, Milton Park, Abingdon, Oxon, OX14 4RN

*CRC Press is an imprint of Taylor & Francis Group, LLC*



*Library of Congress Cataloging-in-Publication Data*
Names: Robinson, Chris, 1967– author
Title: Raw outrage : the films of Phil Mulloy / Chris Robinson.
Description: First edition. | Boca Raton, FL : CRC Press, 2026. | Includes bibliographical references and index.
Identifiers: LCCN 2025024540 (print) | LCCN 2025024541 (ebook) | ISBN 9781032862118 hardback | ISBN 9781032865270 paperback | ISBN 9781003527909 ebook
Subjects: LCSH: Mulloy, Phil—Criticism and interpretation
Classification: LCC NC1766.G72 M8537 2026 (print) | LCC NC1766.G72 (ebook) | DDC 791.43/34—dc23/eng/20250619
LC record available at https://lccn.loc.gov/2025024540
LC ebook record available at https://lccn.loc.gov/2025024541

ISBN: 9781032862118 (hbk)
ISBN: 9781032865270 (pbk)
ISBN: 9781003527909 (ebk)

DOI: 10.1201/9781003527909

Typeset in Times
by codeMantra

*Well, for starters, I kinda think Phil Mulloy is the most entertaining—"interesting"—"engaging"—not to mention the most viscerally enjoyable animator since, oh, Tex Avery…okay?*

*His works are primitive in the very best sense of the term, and I'm not talking "neo"-primitive: I mean every bit as primitive as the Three Stooges. Simple? Basic?… like a stick-figure version of Sam Beckett.*

*When it comes to shitpissdoodooweewee—not to mention pustules, scuzz and scum—P.M. is a beacon in the night. The Ubu Gang? They're a pack of art school aesthetes—yuppie performance artists—Dada opportunists—by comparison. Pikers!*

Richard Meltzer, *Phil Mulloy: An Appreciation*

# Contents

# Shake 'Em All Down—Introducing Phil Mulloy

Phil Mulloy is the punk bluesman of animation. His films are short, simple, yet profound, and often filled with rage against dehumanizing systems. If Disney represents the heart of animation, then Mulloy is its bowels. Or wait… maybe it's the other way around. Either way, Mulloy's work stands in stark contrast to the soulless, colorful, cartoony world of bunny rabbits, cuddly ogres, and other assorted sexless, wide-eyed moral crusaders who make the world safer and more linear for us. Mulloy's films are deceptively crude, intentionally primitive animation that confronts societal norms with sharp, biting satire.

Mulloy's animations are drawn with thick, bold black lines, featuring stick-figure characters with black skulls, white eyes, and what looks like a flaccid penis for a nose. His tales are laced with cynicism and sarcasm, tackling the world's social, political, and religious contradictions, as well as the repressive and often cruel effects these have on human nature.

I can't recall whether it was 1992 or 1994. It doesn't really matter. It was one of those years, one of those Ottawa International Animation Festivals. I had just begun my journey into animation. Back then, I knew so little—maybe I know even less now than I did then. What I do know is that I used to get so much more excited about the films being submitted. These days, after 34 years in animation, that body buzz is rare. Part of it comes from being around so long that surprises are fewer and farther between. But it's more than that.

I've always been drawn to minimalist, raw, punk-inspired, sketch-style works. Back in those early days, the films that blew my mind were the works of Phil Mulloy. I know it was one of the *Cowboys* films I saw for the first time, and I was immediately smitten. It was everything most animation was not: roughly drawn, with black stick-figure characters sporting penis-shaped heads. These films were violent, crass, and yet sharp critiques of societal ills and hypocrisies. Watching Mulloy's films—remember, this was pre-internet, before YouTube, behind-the-scenes videos, teasers, or social media hype—was revelatory. It felt like the first time I heard punk or felt the raw power of The Who. It was an untamed rage that mirrored my own feelings about society.

Every festival year, I looked forward to seeing a new Mulloy film. That excitement lasted well into the 2000s. But then animation changed. Mulloy made fewer films. That said, he did create three polarizing features during that time—about as minimalist as animation could get, even bordering on anti-animation. Derek Jarman's *Blue* might still hold the crown for extreme minimalism, but Mulloy's features were close contenders. I remember Ottawa audiences being deeply divided. Yet, incredibly, all three of those features won Grand Prizes at Ottawa in the first decade of the 2000s. I still can't explain how. Each jury was different, as was each audience. These were not easy films for viewers accustomed to Disney's linear dreamscapes. One year, people even booed when his feature *Dead Not Buried* won. I was delighted. I love when juries go against the grain and make passionate, honest decisions like that.

After that last feature, for various professional and personal reasons, Mulloy's output dwindled. The Channel 4 era of animation funding and exhibition was long gone. Meanwhile, animation as a medium evolved. Thousands more shorts were being produced annually, and the tone shifted. Previously overlooked themes—mental health, addiction, abuse, autism, ADHD, sexuality—finally began to take center stage. This was necessary and welcome, but, over time, these themes became dominant. It felt like every other film dealt with anxiety or OCD, though not always in compelling ways.

As the world plunged into chaos—pandemics, wars, genocides, conspiracy theories—it seemed animators struggled to address the complexities of reality. Maybe they didn't want to. Maybe they were too scared, retreating inward. In recent years, I've found myself longing for works like Phil Mulloy's—bold films that critique religion, masculinity, class, nationalism, war, racism, and xenophobia. Mulloy's films aren't perfect; they can feel restrictive. But that's the beauty of punk: spit it all out and see what happens.

Recently, Mulloy has quietly resurfaced on the festival circuit with potent shorts like *Endgame* and *Once Upon a Time on Earth*. The latter, perhaps his most earnest work, is notably less satirical. Around this time, I felt an itch to revisit his films, to reintroduce them to a generation that never experienced them firsthand.

Then, in 2024, I learned that Animafest Zagreb was organizing a major tribute to Mulloy, complete with screenings, an exhibition, and a talk. That was the spark. Even though I'd promised myself my book on Lewis Klahr would be my last on animation, I knew it was time to write this one.

What follows is a chronological journey through Mulloy's career. It combines my thoughts on each film, Mulloy's insights into their origins, and glimpses of his biography. My hope is that this book inspires readers to seek out his works (yes, some are on Vimeo and YouTube) and feel the excitement I felt when first encountering his blistering critiques of societal contradictions, hypocrisies, and cruelties.

Because let's face it: it's not us versus them. It's all of us. The 1% and the 99%. We are all complicit in the world we've created, and we are all responsible for trying to fix it. I'd even argue that the rise of films tackling personal, internal struggles like mental health is a reflection of the hyper-capitalist, dog-eat-dog system we've been groomed for. Fix the system, and maybe those anxieties, that depression, that OCD, and ADHD might ease, too.

Big thanks first and foremost to my colleagues at Animafest Zagreb for the unintended inspiration to do this: Daniel Šuljić, Matea Milić, Paola Orlić, and Ornela Čop.

Thanks also to Anastasyia Verlinska, Yiorgos Tsangaris, Devin Hartley, Kelly Neall, Tom McSorley, Tom Knott, Gerben Schermer, Nikica Gilić, Otto Alder, Andreas Hykade, Thomas Meyer-Hermann, David Cuevas, Richard Meltzer, the late Peter Dougherty, and Sean Connelly (CRC Press).

And finally, a massive thanks to Phil Mulloy for giving up a lot of time for interviews, film links, and endless emails from me.

Sadly, Phil passed away on July 10, 2025. I'm sure he is stirring up shit wherever he is now. Thank you Phil for shaking, rattling, and strangling the cozy world of animation.

Thou Shalt Not Bear False Witness

# It's Not Exactly Walt Disney—The Early Years

# 1

When I first met Phil Mulloy in the mid-1990s, I was taken aback. The man before me was well-dressed and soft-spoken (albeit deeply sarcastic). He looked like a polite, middle-class guy who might live in the countryside and work at a bank or something. He sure as hell didn't look like the creator of those minimalist, raw, punk-inspired stick-figure animation rants about society, politics, religion, and gender. So, just how the heck did all this happen?

Mulloy hails from Wallasey, a small town near Liverpool, and describes his upbringing with a mix of fondness and realism. "I come from the wrong

Phil Mulloy

DOI: 10.1201/9781003527909-1

side of Wallasey—not quite at the docks, but near enough," he reflects. His father, an Irish immigrant, moved from Ireland to Liverpool, crossed the River Mersey, and settled in Wallasey. "That's where I was born," Mulloy says. "My father wasn't a docker; he worked on building sites, putting in the sewage pipes."

[1]His father's roots trace back to Achill Island, a remote and rugged place off the west coast of Ireland in County Mayo. "It's a small island—not a great place to live in winter," Mulloy remarks. "There are hardly any trees, just horizontal rain coming at you from the Atlantic. It was quite a hard place, and my father was a hard man. In Summer though it was completely different. Huge skies, and empty beaches, a great place for kids to mess around in. My brother and I spent long days in the rock pools looking for fishes and eels. We loved it there."

Mulloy's mother, a protestant, had married an Irishman, a Catholic. Her side of the family was all lower middle class, teachers, office workers. One was even a bank manager.

> My father's side were farmers with very small plots of land, and landless labourers. For them, times were hard. Most adults had to go to England to make money. Of course at that time being an Irish immigrant wasn't easy. Signs like No Blacks, No Dogs, No Irish, hung in the windows of rooms to rent, summed up the attitude of many at the time.

Mulloy's mother was left to raise two children while his father spent much of his time with his fellow Irish workers at the pub. "He liked the company of his mates, and spent a lot of his time there," Mulloy says, "He worked hard and drank hard."

Mulloy admits that he rarely remembers seeing his father much and that later in life they remained somewhat estranged… "I don't think my mother knew what she'd let herself in for. She was left to raise two children pretty much on her own."

In spite of it all, Mulloy recalls having a relatively happy childhood. "You could walk out of the front door and play football out on the street and there was a park up the road, and of course there were always lots of kids to play with. It was a good childhood, but tough. I never looked tough, but I was mixing with kids from all sorts of backgrounds. It wasn't a middle-class upbringing."

The family lived in terraced houses, a defining feature of the northern English landscape. "There are a lot of terraced houses," Mulloy says, "like in the East End of London—just rows and rows of houses, no trees. When I go back there now, the houses are painted blood red. It was a feeder town for the docks and shipbuilders in Birkenhead. That's where I went to school."

Mulloy isn't entirely sure where his interest in art came from, but he thinks it might have been an aunt who was an infant school headmistress.

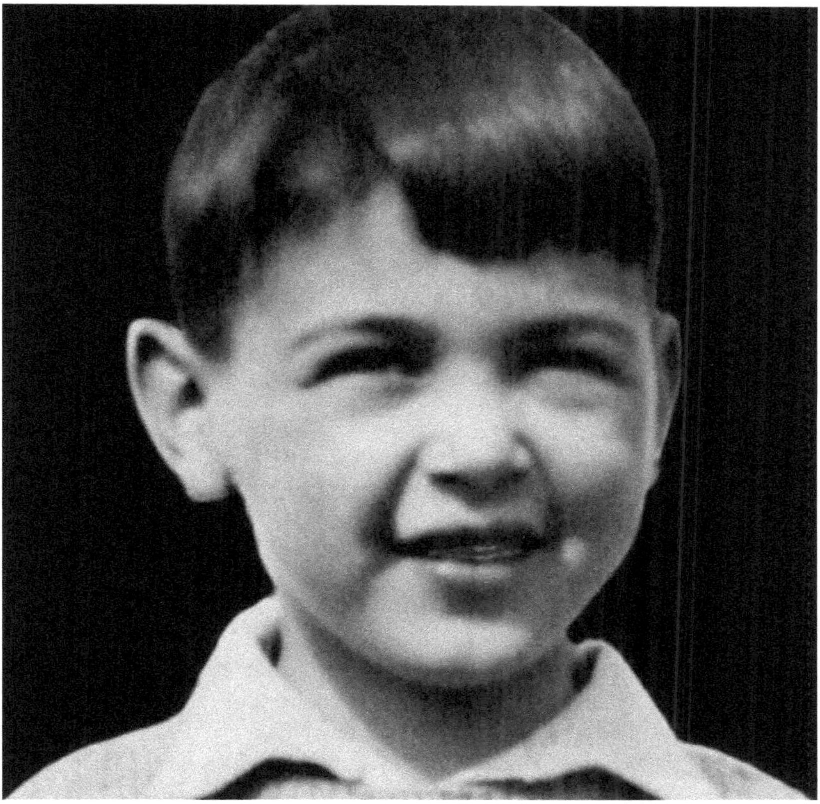

Phil Mulloy, Age 5

"She painted bowls of flowers. I remember her house used to smell of oil paint," recalls Mulloy, "I always enjoyed drawing and painting."

Somewhat surprisingly, given his anti-establishment oeuvre, cartoons, especially Walt Disney, had a significant influence on his early drawings, recalls Mulloy.

> When you're around eight and nine years old, you start copying grown-up drawings. It tends to happen fairly naturally. At some point the child begins to think that their drawings are childish, that is rubbish, and starts copying cartoons. Drawing cartoons is relatively easy, and, of course, it's what adults do. These cartoons were, and still are everywhere, and so it's the same today. Kids quickly put themselves into artistic straight jackets, and then they find these jackets are really quite difficult to take off. I was no different.

Mulloy's journey into art began in a somewhat unconventional way. "When I was in primary school, I passed my exam. That was another thing—people always expected me to do alright," he shared. Mulloy stood out as a bright student, starting to read very early and even reading to his class. Born on August 29th, he was always the youngest in his year, beginning his schooling in September.

However, his transition to St. Anselm's College at age 11 marked a harsh shift:

> It was run by the Irish Christian Brothers. The name Christian means that they were the followers of Christ, but nowhere in the New Testament did I find any talk of the beating of children to improve their education. Most of these men were vicious. I cannot speak for all the kids that passed through their hands, but for my own part and many of those around me learning was accompanied by the daily fear of being hit. Looking back, I cannot help thinking that the presence of a woman in many of their lives might have helped make them more sensitive to the needs of others. By the time I was sixteen, I was desperate to get out of the place.

Amidst this turbulent backdrop, Mulloy began to consider a path in art. After excelling in his O Levels (now GCSEs) with 11 passes, he initially planned to pursue A Levels and go to university. However, his brother's enrollment in art school influenced him to take A Level art a year early and leave before he took his other subjects. After one year, he left St. Anselm and joined a local art college in Wallasey.

"Going to Art College in Wallasey was fantastic," Mulloy recalled. "I felt free for the first time. The contrast between the strict discipline and brutality of St. Anselm's and the sense of liberation I felt at the Art College was stark." He recounted a particularly traumatic incident at St. Anselm's when a Christian Brother lined up the whole class and beat them with a stick for no reason. His backside was left black and blue.

> The guy who did it died the following year. He got his cassock caught up in a tractor and was dragged into it. We went to his funeral, happy that would we would never see him again. Our somewhat shocking indifference to his death was the sad result of this holy man's somewhat primitive teaching methods.

At Wallasey, Mulloy began experimenting with his art.

> I found a lot of tins of water based paint from a second-hand shop...The colours were all brilliant blues, reds, and yellows. I remember the tins had no labels on them, so I was never able to buy them again, but they were, and in some ways still are in my mind, the best paints I ever used. My new sense of freedom to paint whatever I wanted was exhilarating. One of my early works was of people falling from the sky into Hell,

he said. "I was still haunted by religious subjects, particularly the cruelty on display within Christian iconography. A friend later remarked, when he saw one of my animated films, that the film's imagery bore a strong resemblance to these early paintings."

During a trip to Paris with a friend, Mulloy went to see an exhibition of Picasso's work. Inspired, he began painting on wood, using doors and cutting them into shapes that became his personal icons. Unfortunately, most of his paintings from this time were lost.

Mulloy's early years in art college were marked by rebellion and introspection. "I nearly got expelled from Wallasey Art College. My friend and I were asked to do a large painting together. We didn't know what we were doing and laughed at the idea of having to work on the same painting together. We tried to paint something we thought they might like but couldn't agree on anything. Eventually we destroyed the painting and got sent home. I was suspended for about a month. The suspension turned out to be a blessing in disguise. At home, I started working harder than ever. I was determined to succeed."

Reflecting on his transition from painting to film-making, Mulloy recalls the alienation he felt within the art world:

> While studying at Ravensbourne Art College I made two animated films. At the time, I was questioning whether painting was the right path for me. While I enjoyed the act of painting, I felt alienated by the gallery world. The galleries I visited in London seemed distant and detached from my life and experiences. To a nineteen-year-old from the suburbs of Liverpool, they felt like cold, empty spaces where people spoke in hushed, reverent tones, very much like being back in church. Eventually, I gave up painting and started searching for a different way to work creatively. I didn't know exactly what I was looking for, but I knew it had to feel more in tune with my own way of thinking and resonate with a broader, more relatable audience.

This disconnect led Mulloy to question his path. "I started thinking: 'I'm supposed to be painting for these people, but they aren't the people I know. They're not the people I come from.' It was a completely different world," he says.

> In Liverpool, there were bands and groups who spoke directly to the same class of people who listened to their music. But with painting, I felt like I was communicating with a world that was alien to me. There were no galleries in my world, not in my neighborhood. What we did have were cinemas—cinemas everywhere.

Meanwhile, Mulloy had been writing scripts, but he wasn't particularly pleased with the results. "I was never happy with it," Mulloy shares. "I never felt in control until I started doing animation." It was during this time that Mulloy discovered an animation rostrum hidden behind a closed door. Intrigued, he decided to give animation a whirl.

> I bought two 100ft rolls of film and made two pretty awful films—one using the rostrum and another involving a real suitcase on a beach. Whether I would have continued to pursue animation further, I can't say, but

> something surprising happened: one of those early attempts at animation changed the course of my life.

Mulloy's discovery of a rostrum camera marked a turning point. One of those early films earned him admission to the Royal College of Art (RCA), a move that reshaped his creative trajectory.

Once at RCA though, Mulloy found the isolating and time-consuming experience of making hundreds of frame-by-frame drawings alone in a dark room unappealing. He wouldn't make another animated film for two decades.

At the RCA, Mulloy was exposed to underground cinema and avant-garde influences. "I remember going to the Arts Lab on Euston Road and seeing Michael Snow's *Wavelength.* I remember thinking, 'What the hell is this?' There was also Jeff Keen, who did animation. His films were much closer to what I liked," he recalls.

> They felt open—like you could actually make them yourself. You didn't need a big crew or loads of money to make a film. You could do something simple and direct. This was "experimental film-making" made by "underground film-makers", an approach that proved a crucial stepping stone for me. This approach to film-making was totally empowering. The idea that films could be made outside the Film Industry made me believe that I could do something in film. The word experimental was exciting in itself. Here was an arena in which new filmic ideas could be tried out, mistakes made, and perhaps even a good film made.

Mulloy's first film (and the only one to survive from this time period), *Allow Me* (or *Allow Me to Stick It In*, as the opening film credits reveal, 1970), was created during his time at the RCA. "We students were given a 100-foot roll of film and told to go out and make a short film," Mulloy recalled. "I made no real plans for the film—I just chose a few different locations to shoot."

*Allow Me* is a live-action film with a few seconds of haphazard spaghetti animation, yet the snarky Mulloy vibe and gloomy atmosphere are already present. His distinctive style and tone emerge from the very start—albeit in a more convoluted and formally ambitious manner—mixing live act.

A long shot of an apartment building is accompanied by a constant, pulsating thump—reminiscent of footsteps, perhaps those of a woman and child. A voice commands, "Run." Meanwhile, a smoking man cleans a window from the outside. Intermittent snippets of a woman's and a child's voices, alongside a woman speaking on the phone and the previously mentioned spaghetti animation, add to the disjointed auditory tapestry.

A dark, claustrophobic, and menacing aura pervades the film. Is the window cleaner a threat to the unseen woman? The gated curtain transforms into something resembling a spider web or a goalie net—a trap that soon dominates the screen as the thumping soundtrack intensifies. Although rough

Allow Me

around the edges, *Allow Me* already showcases Mulloy's penchant for minimalism and menace, hinting at his broader societal concerns about urban isolation.

"The really important point for me occurred in the editing when I could see the footage and began making the soundtrack," says Mulloy. "It was then that I began putting the disparate fragments together."

Sound was, and remains, an essential element of Mulloy's work. For the phone calls in *Allow Me*, he contacted a few real people and recorded their responses. When someone answered, Mulloy stayed silent. "The people on the other end of the phone would ask questions like, 'Bob, is that you?' or simply call out, 'Hello,' in an increasingly demanding way," he recalls. "I remember feeling pretty guilty about doing it, but the responses gave the film a particular feel—one of individuals calling out in the darkness."

The continual thumping sound was an accident that occurred when his sound recording device kept banging against his leg as he walked. Rather than discard the noise, he decided to use it. "The movement created a rhythmic sound, which sped up as I walked faster," recalls Mulloy. "This speeding up, perhaps, adds a thriller effect to the film. For me, though, it was seen as the oncoming of something chaotic and uncontrollable, heightened by the grid-like curtains on the window and the camera swinging across the ugly concrete buildings."

Mulloy admits that his time at RCA was a mix of both inspiration and disillusionment.

> My original excitement with experimental film dissipated into purely formal visual exercises. For me, my film-making had reached a dead end. I had always worked more intuitively. Now my attempts to take a more intellectual approach had taken me up a blind alley. These moments of self doubt plagued my college life. No, I didn't know where I was going creatively, and certainly didn't have a clue where I'd end up.

Things changed when future film scholar Noël Burch began teaching in the College. For Mulloy, Burch injected some much needed fresh air into the school.

> It was the direction of his analysis, the way he spoke about the films that was so interesting. Here was a way for me to bring narrative back into my films, a way forward. Using narrative, deconstructing narrative, or reworking it—film-makers like Godard were remaking mainstream cinema afresh and with a critical eye.

After graduating, Mulloy began working part-time as a kind of art therapist at a local hospital. "There was one student, a Vietnamese guy who had fought and escaped from the Vietnam War. Mostly, we just talked. It wasn't exactly demanding, but it brought in a little money," he recalls. At the same time, he was making a live-action short, *History and the City* (1977). "I got some funding from the Arts Council and made a film," Mulloy says.

During this period, he joined a collective formed by a group of RCA students. "We used to meet daily to discuss making a film," he says. The group met for about a year and eventually secured funding from the British Film Institute (BFI) to produce a project. However, the process became frustrating for him. "All we did was talk, and nothing was actually happening," he explains.

Eventually, he made the difficult decision to leave, despite his previous work playing a significant role in securing the funding. "They went on to make the film without me," he notes.

Mulloy never aspired to enter the traditional film industry. "I always intended to make my own live-action films. Animation was not even a consideration. When I left the RCA, I had completely forgotten—I just wanted to make films," he states.

Shortly after, Mulloy began working on a live-action feature, *In the Forest* (1978), a film set entirely in a woodland setting but depicting the journey of three peasants through British history. "It was not a conventional historical drama but a fragmentary mix of real historical moments with imaginative re-enactments."

Mulloy's creative path has always been intertwined with the political and cultural currents of his time. Reflecting on the politically charged atmosphere of his early years, he recalls, "Yeah, that was the feeling at the time. You felt that things were going to change for the better and that you'd be part of that change. Conversations with friends were all like that."

Mulloy spent the rest of the 1970s and most of the 1980s making live-action films and documentaries that were screened on TV. However, he grew frustrated with the long creative process of writing scripts and then waiting for financing for those scripts. Sometime in 1988, while awaiting word on a funding proposal, Mulloy started drawing for the first time in almost 20 years. His wife, Vera Neubauer, a film-maker and animator in her own right, suggested that he make a film from the drawings. "I did, and the feeling of drawing and painting rekindled the pleasure that had originally led me to art school all those years before," he says. "The great thing was that all I needed was A4 sheets of paper and a 16mm camera. I had both, so I went ahead. Instead of staring at words on a sheet of A4 paper, I began covering these same pages with imagery."

Freed from scriptwriting, Mulloy dove straight into drawing and animating. "I let my drawings guide me as I worked. I felt as though I could do anything I liked. I no longer had to please anyone. Not knowing where I was going was totally liberating. Best of all, I didn't have to give a damn about what producers or TV executives thought."

The experience marked a turning point for Mulloy—not just in his artistic path but also in his content.

As Clare Kitson notes in her book *British Animation: The Channel 4 Factor*:

> Apart from the pleasure of drawing, and the recognition that his political anger could just as well be expressed in this medium as in live action, he saw that without actors or crew to pay, it would also be cheaper to produce and therefore perhaps more attractive to funding bodies.[2]

Mulloy's drawings for what eventually became *Eye of the Storm* (1989), his animation debut, were inspired by a series of haunting photos he encountered as a child of Russian peasants hanged by their German captors. The photos had a profound effect on Mulloy. As he told Clare Kitson, "It was a moment in which I lost a certain aspect of my own innocence. The images I created were a poetic meditation upon this moment."

*Eye of the Storm* (1989) opens with a man's scream—one that sounds like Mulloy's own voice—as a boy awakens, "It is midnight. Mummy and Daddy are asleep, and I walk the house like a murderer." A live-action shot captures a candle and the boy's face, showing him disturbed by the sounds outside, particularly the wind. Suddenly, a flurry of animated drawings—Mulloy's

Eye of the Storm

distinctive rough black ink on white paper—races across the screen, as if portraying the jumbled thoughts of a sleepy, anxious child.

As the boy roams his cave-like house, he encounters drawings—possibly his own—followed by old photographs. Then the menacing drawings return, seemingly illustrating the lives of long-gone figures: images of a war that once terrified the English (Mulloy himself was a post-war baby). The film touches on disturbing themes, including unsettling sexual imagery (a reference to "a stiffened penis" and perhaps a rich kid aroused by violence) and shocking visuals like papers glued on with human semen, along with a reference to Jews being hanged. This raises the question: did something traumatic happen in this house, or was it the effect of a photograph that scarred the young Mulloy?

The film evokes the semi-conscious night terrors familiar to many children—where everyday sounds are magnified in an anxious mind. The drawings themselves are unrestrained visions of horror, depicting death, murder, destruction, and explosions.

As a child, Mulloy sometimes scoured through his father's Sunday newspaper, *The News of the World*. Reading about German and Japanese concentration camps sickened him.

> The film for me was about the first moment I came in contact with the disgusting things people could do to one another. It was about the loss of innocence. Of course, being brought up a Catholic, I had become familiar with images of brutality and horror, but the blurry images of emaciated people

Possession

> in the paper were something different. These people were real, not painted statues. How does a child make sense of such things? And of course, there were pictures of Hiroshima and Nagasaki, and the fear of nuclear war. I was eleven years old, standing in the school playground, almost paralysed with fear. What was the third secret delivered by Our Lady to the children at Fatima? Was it that the world was ending? This film was not just a record of that moment but an expression of the fear I felt—and, to no small degree, the fear I have continued to feel.

Mulloy began making *Possession* (1990) during a chaotic and hectic period. Along with his wife, Vera, and their children, he moved from London to West Wales. Reflecting on that time, he recalled:

"We had settled on a smallholding deep in the countryside, on which there were a few sheds. One of them, an old cowshed, became our workspace, and for the next nine years, we both worked there."

He chose *Red Riding Hood* as a template because of its universal familiarity:

> Everybody knows the story, so I did not have to retell it. I would just use the characters and give them similar but different roles. For instance, the woodcutter—who eventually kills the wolf—would be the destroyer of the forest, the rich capitalist, and the bringer of order. The wolf would represent chaos. Red Riding Hood would still be the victim, but she would side with the wolf against her father. There would be an attempt to tell a story, but because of the chaos, it would fail.

Mulloy thrived during this process. Animation freed him from the creative shackles of scripts and storyboards:

> Making animation in this way, for me, is both dull and boring. My background in art drove me to reject that approach. My focus was on speed—how quickly I could get ideas out of my head and onto paper. Each day, I'd step into the cowshed and start experimenting with different techniques: ink, paint, charcoal—anything that could leave a mark. The texture and intensity of the marks mattered more than their appearance. I'd tear the paper, piece it back together, and layer over it. For me, the work itself—and the process of making it—was the main thing. The doubts, the dead ends, the rough, unfinished rawness of the work were all integral to the final piece. It wasn't about making something polished; it was about foregrounding the process, capturing the thing itself—capturing the Wolf. After spending nearly fifteen years sitting quietly at a typewriter or computer, this way of working was entirely different. It was a release—an act of both creation and destruction.

A recurring theme in Mulloy's work is humanity's inhumanity toward itself. "Although I no longer consider myself a Catholic, growing up in the Catholic Church, I held onto the principle: 'Do unto others as you would have done unto yourself,'" he reflects.

> It affected me. Then you'd see newspapers filled with images of people in concentration camps, placed right next to pages with sex. It was all mixed together, almost like titillation. I used to put myself in the way of these things—reading horror books as a kid. I remember one about a failed assassination attempt on Louis XIV. His punishment was gruesome, with people wounding him and pouring sulfur into his wounds. It was in Paris, with crowds watching and cheering. And then there were the lives of the martyrs in the Roman amphitheaters. That sort of thing was always around, and it gave me a bleak view of people. Religion taught that suffering leads to heaven, but at some point, I stopped believing in that. I tried replacing it with Marxism—creating heaven on earth—but that doesn't work.

Mulloy admits that his view of humanity grew increasingly bleak—partly triggered by the rise of Margaret Thatcher to power. He recalls hearing her declare, "There's no society, only individuals," and reflects:

> The films I made in the late '80s and early '90s were shocking. My films depicted the terrible things that people did to each other. I was shocked and I wanted the audience to be shocked. People were becoming more individualistic, the acquisition of money by the few to the detriment of the many had become the watchword. The cruelty that this engendered, the disregard of the welfare of others became the subject of my films. In some respects I wanted the short sharp films to act as a warning about where British society was heading. You didn't see films like that often, except maybe in punk work. I was impressed by punk art—the fanzines, the creativity, the punks ability to make something almost out of nothing.

*Possession* also marks the debut of Romanian composer Alex Balanescu in Mulloy's films.

"There was a film-maker friend—a friend of Vera's, a Swiss woman living in London," Mulloy recalls. I remember asking her if she knew good violin players. She said, "Yeah, Alex Balanescu. He's a brilliant violinist, classically trained at Juilliard School in New York, yet influenced by multiple musical styles. He's very willing to experiment and plays the violin in ways that other violinists would not."

The two men met and Mulloy showed Balanescu a cut of *Possession*. Balanescu liked it and agreed to collaborate. That initial meeting sparked a fruitful collaboration. In addition to *Possession*, Balanescu provided music for the *Cowboys* series, *The Sound of Music*, *Thou Shalt Not Kill* (from *The Ten Commandments* series), *The History of the World* series, and the animated documentary inspired by his life, *The Winds of Change*.

For many, these early films remain largely undiscovered—even Mulloy himself had nearly forgotten them. But in 2024, as he prepared for a career retrospective and a lifetime achievement award at Animafest Zagreb, he began revisiting his early work. My persistence in urging him to review everything for this book may have played a role as well.

Tinfish

After revisiting *Possession*, Mulloy decided to work on restoring the original film.

> I never really showed it to anybody, although looking at it now, I think it's really quite strong. For me, its strength lies in seeing the obvious enjoyment I had while making it—feeling free and trying to find my way through that freedom. The music by Alex Balanescu is fantastic and Benat Achiery sings beautifully. The violin of Balanescu and Achery's voice make for an exciting combination.

Although Mulloy is hazy about its origins and production year, *Tinfish* (1990) marks another important turning point. It signalled both a shift in style and a change in format. If *Eye of the Storm* and *Possession* were, to borrow a musical analogy, like EPs or albums, *Tinfish* (which in British naval slang for torpedo) explodes onto the screen like a punk single—imagine a cross between GG Allin, Hubert Selby Jr., and Saul Steinberg on an acid trip.

Funded by the British Arts Council and the BBC's *The Late Show*, *Tinfish* is a rapid-fire visual and tonal ink-and-paper explosion that hastily summarizes the origin of the species. A sign announces "In the Beginning," and from there, themes of evolution, love, power, work, and the fruits of labor unfold. Essentially, it is Mulloy's summary of existence in a capitalist society.

A fish swims and is eaten by a bigger fish, which in turn is eaten by an even bigger fish. After evolution, we discover love and one another, but that love transforms into procreation and a labor force/consumer base. From there, evolution devolves into a scattered mélange of miserable, exploited consumers—leading to protest, conflict, war, and one massive explosion. Mulloy portrays evolution not as a natural process but as something hijacked or co-opted by those in power, turning us into nothing more than breeding consumer twits. Remarkably, although he made this bullet-paced blast in 1990, watching it in 2025, it feels—unfortunately—as fresh, accurate, and depressing as ever.

"That's because it comes from a real place," he concludes. "Most of my work stems from strong feelings—whether it's anger or frustration at how people are treated. That emotion was the driving force behind those films."

While Mulloy can't recall exactly how he was feeling during the creation of *Tinfish*, he knows he was angry.

> Britain had changed—people were getting rich in the financial sector, and Thatcher had wanted to crush the unions, and in many ways had succeeded. That feeling of the time shaped my work. Margaret Thatcher's government in the 1970s was a turning point for me—it shaped my perspective.

With *Tinfish*, Mulloy begins to carve out a more defined narrative—a trend that would continue in his 1990s classics such as *Cowboys, Ten Commandments, Great Moments in Film, Laughing Moon,* and *The History of the World.*

The idea of catharsis in creation might sound clichéd, but the violence and rage that seep through Mulloy's process and content—even up to today—make one wonder if the aggressive act of creating was therapeutic in some small way.

"Yeah, it must have been," Mulloy admits.

> But I wasn't thinking about that at the time. The real release was simply not writing any more; it was just enjoying myself Instead of thinking I had to sit there and make money by creating films that people might want to see on television, I was creating primarily for myself. Far away in Wales, I began making films that I liked. I didn't have to give a fig about what a TV audience might like. I began living in the hope that somewhere out in the world there might be an audience that might also like them.

Living in the countryside was liberating for Mulloy and took him back to the early joys of his art college days.

> Enjoying myself really was the release. There was also that sense of control, where you're not being told what to do or how to do it. I wasn't reading books about scriptwriting or trying to fit into industry expectations—that was killing my creativity. Learning to be creative again was thrilling. The fact that some people liked what I was doing was amazing—it made me want to carry on.

Mulloy's approach to film-making radically changed when he began drawing.

> When I started working on thin A4 sheets of paper, I noticed that when the ink hit the paper, parts of it would begin to pucker up. What should I do about it? I decided not to do anything. It was a natural occurrence, a result of the liquid's action on the paper. Some would say that such a mistake should be corrected, but I decided that any mistake should be left in place. I also resolved that the first drawing I made would always be the one I used—nothing would be redrawn. This eliminated any idea of a drawing being 'good' or 'bad.' The drawing was simply what it was. Of course, not every rule can be followed 100 percent of the time, but for the next few years, I adhered to that rule pretty religiously.

Alongside disturbing historical and religious imagery and politics, music has played a significant role in Mulloy's life and work. Music even led him to explore making short films.

> I really liked blues. My brother sang with Howlin' Wolf—what a voice! I remember him singing in the Cavern Club. I like those songs—they're short. You can make music from just a piece of wood and a few bits of string and still convey something powerful. That's how I see my work—the simplicity, the directness, and yet the intensity.

Me, Tony, God, the President, and a Dog

Although it was with *Cowboys* that we first see Mulloy's distinctive skeletal characters, he acknowledges the influence of woodcut imagery on his overall design:

> In the mid-eighties, I had spent many months in the reading room of the British Museum researching a script about one of the leaders of the Leveller Movement in the English Civil War. I came across the woodcut images they had used in their pamphlets. These simple, almost childlike images possessed a strength that still impresses me today. They might not be considered 'great art' in the conventional sense, but they have a strength and sense of urgency that captures the turmoil of the time—or, in the language of that time, 'the world turned upside down.' Around the same time, I saw the *Day of the Dead* exhibition at the Museum of Mankind in London. The liveliness and vibrancy of what was depicted belied the sombre subject matter. Moreover, it was totally irreverent. What appealed to me about both of these styles was their playfulness, their humor, and mostly their fearless disregard for conventional ideas.

Now that his artistic warm-ups were complete, Mulloy jumped fully into animation and, over the next decade, created some of the most groundbreaking and provocative works in international animation. (Disney—this wasn't, nor ever would be, his style, thankfully.)

True to Mulloy's modest, direct approach, he summarizes these early years succinctly: "Honestly, I didn't know what the fuck I was doing. But I really enjoyed it. I worked hard, and that's something I've always done."

## NOTES

1 Unless otherwise noted, all Mulloy quotes in this book are from interviews with the Author, February 2025.

2 Clare Kitson, *British Animation: The Channel 4 Factor* (Bloomington: Indiana University Press, 2009), p. 143.

# "Let Fury Have the Hour[1]"

# 2

The 1990s saw Phil Mulloy firmly established himself in the world of animation with a stream of biting, satirical works that were unlike anything else in the animation landscape. *Cowboys*, *The Sound of Music*, *The Ten Commandments*, *Winds of Change*, *The Chain*, and *The Sexlife of a Chair* remain standouts—important counters to the all-too-often safe, conventional

Cowboys



DOI: 10.1201/9781003527909-2

world of animation. They do so not only through direct commentary on current events but also through a creative process that embraces mistakes, works quickly, and exudes an almost feverish urgency.

## COWBOYS

As mentioned in the introduction *(though you've likely forgotten all about that by now—after all, I imagine you're pausing here and there to scroll on your phone)*, I vividly recall the shock and exhilaration I felt when I first encountered the *Cowboys* films at the Ottawa International Animation Festival in 1992. It was my inaugural year at the festival. I knew nothing about animation, but I was already certain I disliked the sanitized Disney fare—and, indeed, most industry work as well as much of the indie output. Everything felt overly precious; everyone seemed to be trying so hard. *Cowboys* looked as though it had been scribbled by a wonderfully furious lunatic. And, of course, as a neighbor to the U.S., I relished any direct or indirect jabs at what I often referred to as the "special-ed class" among our southern neighbors. There was also a liberating sense that anyone could create such work. While there were far superior examples of animation and design in linear narratives, none matched the intensity, urgency, and satirical fire of *Cowboys*.

The *Cowboys* series (1991) consists of six three-minute films: *Outrage*, *That's Nothin'*, *The Conformist*, *Slim Pickin's*, *Murder!*, and *High Noon*. My initial impression was that the series condemned the U.S.—and all its violent, arrogant, greedy bluster. Although Mulloy was clearly influenced by his love of cowboy movies, the series was really a critique of the absurdity of masculinity. "I used to watch cowboy films as a kid," Mulloy recalled.

> It just seemed like a world of men. It had a lot to do with the women's movement bringing certain things to the forefront. Cowboys are obviously an American thing, but the films weren't just about the U.S. It was more about guys in general—how they behave when they get together. They can be pretty obnoxious.

When starting *Cowboys*, Mulloy asked himself, "What do I want to say about cowboys?" He approached the project episodically. "I might have done one and then thought, 'Oh, I'll do another.' The ideas just came in. The episodic approach feels very natural for animation."

While *Eye of the Storm* and *Possession* were self-funded, Mulloy knew full well he couldn't keep working that way. "I didn't know where I was headed, but I understood that if I wanted to keep making films, I needed to secure funding. That's why the idea of creating a series of short films came to me—but to make that happen, I'd need to create a storyboard for each film in the series."

In his pre-animation career in the early '80s, Mulloy had made two live-action dramas for the British Arts Council. "I had come to know a few people in their film department, which was actively supporting independent animated films at the time," Mulloy recalls. "I decided to take my storyboard for a series called *Cowboys* to them. I was fortunate—they offered me a small amount of funding to bring the series to life."

## *OUTRAGE*

*Outrage*

Bullets fly into the film title, accompanied by the almost drunken-sounding notes of "Home on the Range," before a switch is clicked to initiate both Mulloy's film and the film within it. An audience of skeletal cowboys watches as a man and a woman engage in sex on the screen, while a nearby voyeur is appalled by their display. In a surreal twist, the couple bursts into flames—as does the voyeur's dick. Shocked, he flees and appears to start his own religion devoted to the removal of sex organs, where dicks are severed and vaginas stitched up. Meanwhile, a cowboy races to the village bar to report on the copulating couple. Everyone scrambles to view the spectacle before shouting "DISGUSTING!" in unison. A TV viewer sees the scene, becomes aroused, and decides to cut off his dick.

The film within the film ends. The curtain closes. The entire audience is engaged in an orgy.

The dick, it seems, is mightier than the sword.

The narrative evokes Kierkegaard's musings on the dangerous and irrational nature of the masses, emphasizing how easily public sentiment can be manipulated—a phenomenon that has only intensified in an age of ubiquitous connectivity and endless scrolling. At its core, *Outrage* interrogates American hypocrisy regarding sex. On the one hand, the United States maintains a puritanical façade, extolling God and family values; on the other, it relentlessly produces overtly erotic content—sexualizing young women in music videos, films, and advertisements. This contradiction is evident in the way society simultaneously ignites desire and condemns its expression, as seen in the fetishization of schoolgirl uniforms. Figures like Britney Spears transformed what was once ordinary school attire into an object of erotic allure.

With unfiltered shock and satire, *Outrage* comments on the gullibility of the masses and our often troubling relationship with cinema and television, effectively blurring the line between on-screen reality and our perception of real life.

## *THAT'S NOTHIN'*

In a rowdy bar, cowboys drink, arm wrestle, play pool, and toss darts. Amidst the revelry, one of the dart players casually remarks, "That's nothing." The conversation soon pivots from sports to sex, as the men boast about their various sexual conquests—from oral encounters and experiences of being penetrated to even instances of double penetration. Their escalating bravado culminates in an all-out orgy, during which everyone inexplicably catches fire.

As the debauchery intensifies, everything morphs into a phallic symbol—both literally and figuratively—as all the men sport burning erections. This hyperbolic competition underscores an unrelenting desire to outdo one another, satirizing the absurdity of competitive behavior, particularly in the realms of masculinity and sexism, as evidenced by their boastful recounting of sexual exploits.

That's Nothin'

But fear not, dear reader—*That's Nothin'* offers us a happy ending (or two, to be precise). A group of cowboys races back to their horses and engages in intercourse with them. One horse smiles and closes its eyes, savoring the moment.

"I don't remember men boasting about sex so much when I was older, but in school there were always guys who did," recalls Mulloy.

> They might say, 'I banged her' or, 'Yeah, she was good.' I just took those things and exaggerated them, seeing how far I could push it. I wasn't trying to be shocking—that's just how I am. Sometimes I say things out of line, and Vera will ask, 'Why did you say that?' My son will say, 'Dad, did you realize what you just said to that guy?' And I'll think, 'Oh shit, what did I just say?' Maybe these films are a bit like that—I just say things, and in films, you can get away with it.

## *THE CONFORMIST*

A cowboy rides a wheeled horse across the desert when he spots a real horse. Determined, he embarks on a relentless pursuit—day and night—for ten long years until he finally captures the living animal and rides it. Upon arriving, he

The Conformist

finds himself among cowboys riding modern, four-wheeled horses who laugh at his choice. In a radical act of defiance, he amputates the captured horse's legs, ultimately reverting to riding the wheeled contraption he started with.

In one fell swoop, Mulloy mocks the clash between the natural and the artificial, between tradition and technology, and even our insatiable consumer appetite for the next new fix—even when it isn't truly new. Mulloy could just as easily be commenting on fashion and taste, highlighting the paradoxical desire both to fit in and to stand out.

## *SLIM PICKIN'S*

At a political rally, a crowd chants, "Vote! Slim! Vote!" as signs bearing his name dominate the scene. During his speech, Slim offers extravagant promises of wealth, and the audience eagerly swallows his hollow assurances—each promise drifting away like a bubble.

Slim Pickin's

Suddenly, chaos erupts when a televised fight incites panic, prompting people to dash off with wheelbarrows full of gold and televisions. In the ensuing frenzy, citizens even bathe in gold, despite a warning on TV that cautions, "BEWARE! Someone might take your stuff away."

In response, makeshift fortifications spring up as people scramble to protect their wealth. Amid the turmoil, a man carrying a toy horse appears and confiscates the money—likely the funds Slim diverted to build walls and fortified cities—resulting in Slim ultimately losing everything.

Mulloy uses this scenario to comment on the emptiness of political promises and the scarcity of truly reliable leaders in many countries. He also appears to criticize anti-government and anti-tax advocates who paradoxically make numerous demands on those same institutions.

Clearly, Mulloy has crafted a work of total fiction. Nothing like this is conceivable in reality. I mean, imagine a leader intent on building walls simply to keep others out!

## *MURDER!*

A man shoots two people. Gunmen chase him, firing round after round until he finally runs out of ammo—they grab him and carry him off.

*Murder!*

In the city, a couple sits at home when a newspaper arrives with bold headlines about a hanging—about killing the guy. The masses devour the headlines, and the couple races to the hanging with their baby.

Everyone intervenes—either to stop the hanging or to hasten it.

The baby survives… and rises in the form of a beast… or perhaps the baby is possessed by the spirit of the hanged man.

Violence begets violence—a new generation inherits this brutal legacy from the previous one.

Mulloy succinctly satirizes the perplexing mix of hate and fascination that many harbor toward violence and murder. We claim to condemn it, yet somehow we secretly revel in it. Mulloy suggests that the media plays a significant role in manufacturing this contradictory response through sensationalism—fueling our fixation on murders and other grotesque events.

## HIGH NOON

A pocket watch ticks toward noon. Two men stand ready to duel, while two others pray for them to stop. A grave is dug, and the earth parts between them. Their guns are loaded, and a cigar is stomped out. People race from the bar to watch as eager, beastly, bloodthirsty buzzards gather. A newspaper screams,

*High Noon*

"KILL!" Men at desks shout, "KILL!" Even a baby cries out, "KILL!!"—it's a society drooling for violence.

Yet both duelists sweat—they don't seem to want to die. As night falls, their pants drop and their noses turn red… and everyone laughs. It appears they are mocked for rejecting violence.

In the vein of *Murder!*, Mulloy presents a society where violence is expected, lauded, and anticipated; yet when reason prevails, the masses are disappointed and let down. There is something inherently cruel at work as the crowd laughs at the misfortunes of the shooters—their pants falling, one even sporting a clownish red nose.

*Cowboys* is by no means perfect, but it was never meant to be. Here, an unharnessed Mulloy unleashes his frustration and fury over the world's stupidity. His crude, simplistic drawings perfectly capture the often vile, one-dimensional landscape he critiques—a barren world devoid of nuance or subtlety, almost anticipating the rise of twit leadership. Remarkably and tragically, these films feel as if they could have been made today.

*Cowboys* marked the debut of what became Mulloy's distinctive grotesque character design—his skeletal dickheads (well, that's what I call them).

> I used to go out walking a lot, and I'd let my mind open up. Ideas would come from who knows where. I'd start drawing without knowing where it was going. I remember there was this face I used to draw—kind of a black face

> with teeth. It used to annoy me, so I called it 'my annoyance.' It wasn't quite like the cowboys I ended up drawing, but it was probably something like that. One day I just drew it, and it was a cowboy. And I thought, 'This is it.'

Mulloy also drew on Day of the Dead imagery, and he noted the impact of the drawings by the Italian artist and printmaker Giovanni Domenico Tiepolo (1727–1804). As Mulloy recalled:

> In 1978 I made a feature film called *In The forest*. Two characters in the film wore black masks. The design of the masks were based on the Pulcinella masks used in the drawings of Tiepolo. I remember, one of these characters was featured on the front of a British Film Institute magazine that used to hang around the room I worked in. About thirteen years later, this character popped up again as a basic design for *The Cowboys.*

*Triumph of Pulcinella* by Giovanni Domenico Tiepolo

The decision to continue with black ink and brush was inspired by Japanese calligraphic art. Mulloy loved the energy, stark simplicity, and immediacy expressed in the mark-making. "While drawn animation can be a mind-bendingly boring activity," admits Mulloy, "the work of my partner, Vera, showed me that there were other ways of working—methods that were more dynamic, intuitive, and, importantly, quicker."

Mulloy soon developed a method that enabled him to work simply and fast (each episode took about three months to create). As he told Clare Kitson:

> I tried not to bother about making aesthetic judgments. Black ink painted on paper at speed. Paper cut and ripped out. The image was to be purely

> functional and nothing else. Mistakes were made and left unedited. The films were to have a strong sense of their own materiality. The language the films spoke was to be that of the street rather than the dining room. They were to be moral tales told with an eye and ear for the immoral.[2]

When Mulloy created the six *Cowboys* films, he worked without a strict plan:

> I didn't have all six planned from the start. I've got the book somewhere. It's one of those books you can flick through and see everything. I'd never done that before. I took it along, and they gave me the money—not much, but I made it on 35mm. I had a 35mm rostrum camera that was being thrown out from the place where Vera was teaching, so I got it. It turned out to be a terrible thing to have because it messed up so many films. But it became part of it—the wobbles and everything.

Mulloy was ultimately pleased with the sloppy results:

> I remember trying to do it badly on purpose. I thought, 'If I do it, I won't make mistakes. I won't redo images.' But inevitably, you do. Still, 99% of the time, it was the first take, and I'd accept it. I never re-shot anything unless the rostrum camera overexposed the film, which happened a lot. That camera was awful. Shooting on 35mm, waiting for the film to arrive, and then seeing it all messed up—that was a constant struggle.

Despite these challenges, *Cowboys* found a home on Channel 4. They were shown in late night spots, but that mattered little. At least they have been seen. "Channel 4 was unique, and it doesn't happen anymore, which is a shame," laments Mulloy. "It was a great showcase. But I understand the difficulty of programming odd-length films now. People expect 30-minute or hour-long slots, and broadcasters don't know where to place ads."

While I cannot imagine any of Mulloy's work being shown on television or even most streaming channels today, there was little reaction to Cowboys or any of his subsequent work screened on Channel 4:

> The only time anything got cut was with the second *Intolerance* film. There was a scene of the White House blowing up, and it aired close to 9/11, so they cut it. That was the only time anything of mine was censored. Nowadays, things wouldn't be shown at all. People might be offended, or what you're showing might not be considered suitable for a general audience. But Channel 4 back then was an alternative TV station—they embraced that kind of work.

Reflecting on the evolution of the series, Mulloy explained:

> I just had one idea and then moved on to the next. If someone had asked for *Cowboys Part Two*, I could've come up with more. But I was already using the cowboy theme in *The Ten Commandments*—the same characters, just

> without hats. Otherwise, they were exactly the same, but with a mix of men and women.

The *Cowboys* series also did well on the international festival scene. Major animation festivals like Annecy, Ottawa, and Zagreb screened some of the individual films. Mulloy recalled: "There was a kind of buzz around it. People would come up and either tell me it was shit or say they liked it. Either way, they knew about it, which was good. A little buzz is okay—it means people know who you are and maybe want more."

*Cowboys* became so popular that an ad agency representing Doritos approached him about doing an ad in the same style. Mulloy was both intrigued and baffled by the idea:

> I remember thinking, *Oh my God—Cowboys? In a commercial?* They had some ad concepts written out, but I knew they wouldn't go anywhere. It was such a strange idea. But at the same time, I thought, *Maybe I should get some T-shirts made—just in case something happens with this.* For a moment, I thought it could actually make me money.

It never did.

Still, Mulloy leaned into the absurdity of it all and began creating fake ads. "I decided to create *Cowboys* merchandise," he said. "I made different products—*Cowboy Scent*, for example, which was literally just a bottle of piss. There was also *Cowboy Durex* and a few other things." Among the other fake ads: a Russian Roulette family game ("to help the population explosion," says the ad), a "my little cowboy" doll that plays Mozart, a chocolate bar-shaped penis, Cowboy condoms, etc…

For Mulloy, the unexpected success of *Cowboys* reignited his passion for creating. "Suddenly, people liked what I was doing. People had heard of me. I felt like I'd broken into a new scene—one that allowed me to enjoy painting again, to work with my hands instead of just sitting and typing all the time. And that made me happy."

## *THE SOUND OF MUSIC* (1993)

Car horns, broken windows, dogs barking, and women screaming. Menacing-looking characters wander the city streets, ignoring or growling at one another. In the Swiftian inspired *The Sound of Music*, we see the city through the eyes of Wolf—a window cleaner by day and jazz musician by night. Through each window, Wolf witnesses violence, anger, police brutality,

The Sound of Music

apathy, crime, and killing—a society that punishes one sort of violence but celebrates and craves another (e.g., boxing, dog fighting). Wolf finds it all devastating.

At night, he encounters even more gluttony, theft, cruelty, and hate. Along with preachy, bullshit prayers from the rich—who couldn't care less about the meek and unfortunate—Wolf observes homelessness, rampant consumerism, and charity dinners that benefit no one but the wealthy. He even performs at one of these upscale functions. Wolf drinks and takes pills to keep sane. The staff serve them dirty food; wigs are washed in toilets before being returned to the fancy ladies. There is endless brutality toward animals, with more and more food being shoveled into these gluttonous fucks—until, when the food runs out, they even start killing humans to keep feeding the rich.

Finally, overwrought by the violence and hatred surrounding him, Wolf succumbs. He takes his saxophone and, in a burst of desperate rage, smashes a fat, rich patron to death. Even the seemingly decent will inevitably crumble into a muddled reflection of the society that envelops them.

*The Sound of Music*, originally titled *Eldorado* (the name of both a shop in the film and a fictional city of gold in mythology), is one of Mulloy's most significant works—and if you had to choose a film to represent or summarize his output, this would be it. Mulloy depicts a grotesque, brutal, and inhumane society. Alex Bălănescu's soundtrack effectively skirts between free-form jazz in the beginning—accompanied by a man's howling voice—and more restrained classical sounds in the dining scenes, perfectly complementing Mulloy's dour and ugly designs.

> It was really an expression of my anger. Pure anger," recalls Mulloy. "With Alex playing the music and the way people eat—it was a critique of society and the way things were going. There was no single incident or event that triggered my anger. I think it was more about just observing things.
>
> I remember thinking about window cleaners—how they look into people's homes and see how they live. That idea fascinated me. So in the film, you see them cleaning windows, looking inside, seeing people fighting, starving, just living their lives.

After *Cowboys*, Mulloy had wanted to develop more series but felt nothing would get financed. "I was thinking about Channel 4, and I knew 10 minutes was probably the longest they'd go for," he says. "You're not working in a vacuum—you have to consider what can actually get made. Most animation is short. I'm not Aardman."

Mulloy storyboarded the film, but there were structural changes made along the way. Initially, he intended to include collage or cut-out adverts, but he scrapped the idea when he found that "they weren't funny—they just interrupted the music. Alex's music builds up a head of steam, and the ads just stopped that momentum. The film needed to go all the way to that chaotic, screaming climax, so I dropped the ads."

The urban setting in *The Sound of Music* was shaped by Mulloy's impressions from living in London.

> I wanted to show the city from the outside, with these big blocks of flats. The setting is very much London to me. I used to take the Tube from Brixton, and it's familiar territory—the city where you live. And then uptown in Chelsea, there's this big banquet full of very rich people.

On the technical side, Mulloy recalls,

> I'd have to check, but I think I stuck to the storyboard pretty closely. I mean, I do like working spontaneously, but I probably kept to it. I worked quickly—I wasn't spending a long time on it. It was cutouts, so they just moved, and I could shoot a scene a day. The drawings were quick too.

Clare Kitson recalls that the production was a relatively easy and inexpensive experience (it cost £44,000) and was amicable overall. Surprisingly, *The Sound of Music* aired on Channel 4 with no hassles—somewhat to the chagrin of Kitson, who acknowledged that

> any publicity is better than the stony silence usually encountered by our animation seasons, and knowing that the press was not averse to throwing

> up its hands in horror at the excesses of Channel 4, our press officer phoned around to alert TV critics to the treat they had in store—discreetly suggesting the nature of some of the film's delights.[3]

Unfortunately, aside from a number of sponsors and dignitaries leaving the cinema when the film debuted during the opening night festivities of the Stuttgart International Animation Festival (even Mulloy wanted to walk out when he realized they were screening the film in the wrong format), there were no scandals to help promote the film. In fact, one reviewer hailed the film in a 1995 review of Channel 4 animation shorts:

> It's like a blow-torch in the face. Fashioned in splashes of harsh black ink which just about form jackal-like characters (all clothes-peg teeth and scooped-out sockets), its smudged details sometimes blur into a grey fudge, assuming abstract proportions. There are some gruesomely satisfying set-pieces, such as when a window cleaner vomits from the top of his ladder and hits a bird in mid-flight, which plummets to earth where it is savaged by a mutt who is then, in turn, flattened by a car. The restaurant scenes, where livestock is hacked to death in the kitchens, would have even Ralph Steadman reaching for the smelling salts. It might be about urban decay, or declining hygiene standards. Perhaps it's such a blast because it just doesn't matter what it's about—you're swept along by the vigour and the mischief.[4]

## *LAUGHING MOON* (1993–1994)

For his next project, Phil Mulloy received an unexpected request from MTV Europe's creative director, Peter Dougherty—a major supporter of independent animators including Mulloy (Dougherty loved *Cowboys*)—to pitch ideas for a campaign addressing social injustice. "Peter just asked if I had any ideas for a series, and I said, 'Sure, I'll come up with something.' It wasn't a huge amount of money, but it was something," recalls Mulloy.

Determined to take a different approach from *Cowboys*, Mulloy envisioned a series of roughly half a dozen 30-second shorts, each serving as a sharp, satirical observation on various issues. The seven resulting episodes are blisteringly effective, more hits than misses.

Despite being commissioned for MTV, *The Laughing Moon* shorts retained Mulloy's distinctive voice. "They weren't commercial at all," he confirmed. "They were just me doing whatever I wanted. They weren't meant to sell anything—nobody was going to buy them."

Each segment is set in some surreal, isolated world (it almost looks like the characters are adrift on a planet's landscape) and it ends with the moon, you guessed it, laughing at these idiots. "The idea was to laugh at

Laughing Moon

human existence. It's just a horrible moon laughing at people - at the way they behaved."

One standout episode—arguably one of Mulloy's finest moments—depicts a man running back and forth between two brick walls on a train track, repeatedly banging his head against the wall with no success. After several attempts, he stumbles and falls off the track to avoid an oncoming vehicle. As he rises, he sees a vast forest filled with paths stretching in multiple directions. Overwhelmed, he panics, jumps back onto the track, and resumes running toward the wall.

In just 30 seconds, Mulloy delivers a biting commentary on humanity's fear of freedom. The brick walls serve as a metaphor reminiscent of Plato's Cave, where people mistake shadows for reality. Instead of embracing the endless possibilities beyond the track, the man retreats to the rigid, binary structure he knows. The episode also offers a scathing critique of political systems—particularly in the U.S., U.K., and Canada—where citizens are often trapped between two indistinguishable parties, both serving corporate interests.

In episode 2, set on the moon or some other celestial setting, a king pays for a chair. As he goes to sit, the chair is pulled away, causing him to fall. Injured, he is then charged for crutches and medical care—only to have the crutches taken away and replaced with a wagon as his condition worsens. Eventually, a hand upends the cart, killing him, and there's one final expense: a coffin.

While the episode could be seen as a potential critique of wasted taxes or a fragile healthcare system, Mulloy firmly clears up the mystery of its meaning: “It was just about people paying for crap. They buy something, it’s broken. They replaced it, it’s still crap.” He buys things that hurt him to the point where he dies – and has to pay for his coffin. Someone is always profiting even in death.

Episode 3 presents two fenced-off groups of people, clearly representing nations. They wave their respective flags before war erupts. The conflict escalates into mass slaughter until their ammunition runs out, leaving only the leaders standing atop a mound of corpses.

Episode 4 is a brutally succinct take on smoking: a man smokes, coughs, vomits, and dies.

In episode 5, a gang of Nazis and white nationalists stand on the moon. As they chant *Sieg Heil*, Hitler’s head appears, vomiting out skeleton warriors who proceed to terrorize the world. That is, until the hand of God intervenes, seizing them and flushing them down a toilet into hell.

Episode 6, *The Fight* (1993), features a black and a white boxer pummeling each other in the ring. The audience, growing increasingly frenzied, demands blood. But instead of delivering more violence, the fighters ultimately embrace, kiss, and ascend to heaven, forming a heart. The crowd erupts in boos. People, sadly, are idiots.

Finally, in episode 7, set in a church, two ministers preach to their respective congregations. Their theological debate escalates into physical violence as they attempt to kill each other—until they awaken God, who, much like with the Nazis, flings them both straight to hell.

A recurring theme in *Laughing Moon*—which Mulloy would explore further in *Ten Commandments*—is the oppressive nature of rigid binaries. His characters exist in a world of suffocating polarity, locked in cycles that limit their options and freedoms. As a species, we are complex and contradictory, yet we remain trapped in these narrow frameworks of “either/or,” too afraid—like the man in episode 1—to step off the paths that have been carefully paved for us.

***Great Moments of Film (1995)***, perhaps inspired by the dark and satirical *Cowboys* ads, is a twisted nod to cinema. It also recalls Robin Steele’s *Stick Figure Theatre* animations from the same era, in which Steele used stick figures to reenact famous movie scenes while retaining the original soundtracks.

As expected, Mulloy takes a different approach. In these 30-second segments, he delivers a surreal homage to films like *Jaws*, *Interview with the Vampire*, *Thelma & Louise*, *Dirty Harry* (which features a man sailing a toy boat in his toilet before dunking his own head in), *The Terminator*, and *Taxi Driver.*

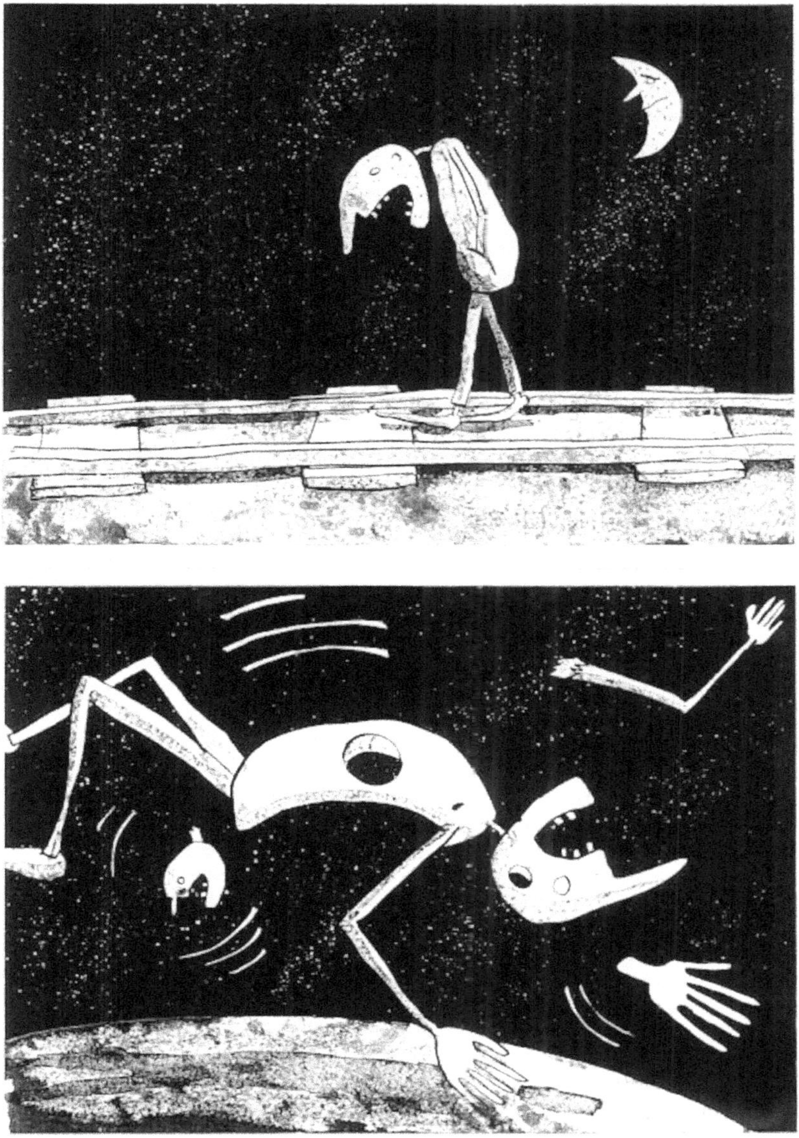

Laughing Moon

Great Moments of Film – Taxi Driver

*Great Moments of Film* was made purely for pleasure. "I was just in the zone," Mulloy recalls. "They were quick to make. The whole thing took about a week. It's nothing fantastic, just short bits."

Armed with the same skeletal figures and minimalist backdrops, *The History of the World* was originally intended to consist of 133 episodes, but only three were ever made. Mulloy explains the project's background: "I got some funding to do one, and I ended up making three. It was another way of thinking about a series, similar to the *Cowboys* ethic, but with different subject matter."

The ironically titled *The Age of Reason Begins* (1993) takes place in Paris during 1793—better known as the Reign of Terror, a period marked by public executions and massacres during the French Revolution. The film presents a series of public beheadings. Then, in a grimly absurd turn, the next victim has his genitals severed by the guillotine. The crowd erupts in applause. A film camera appears, and the newly castrated man is interviewed. He couldn't be happier—he has newfound clarity now that sex is out of the equation. Finally, the severed organ is retrieved from the garbage and sold as "salt and pepper."

In *The Invention of Writing* (1994), Mulloy explores the origins of writers, portraying them as spineless sponges who couldn't get laid. As usual, he cuts through the muck to reveal both the ugliness of truth and the truth of ugliness. Oh, and it's pretty damn funny—in that cringey, uncomfortable way. Think *The Far Side* meets *Monty Python* in Ralph Steadman's studio.

The film with a woman revealing her "bush" to a man (referred to as "the loser"). He becomes aroused, but there's always another man with a bigger penis standing behind him, ready to beat the crap out of him. The victor claims the woman, and the cycle repeats—until *the loser* finally has a revelation. In frustration, he rips off his own penis, dips it into a bottle of ink, and begins to write: *The pen(is) mightier than the sword.* His newfound talent wins him admiration from women, who worship him like groupies. The other men, unable to compete, grow furious and beat him senseless.

Then, in a sudden and jarring cut, the film shifts to a postcard, then to an image of Hiroshima, as a voice—presumably that of the Enola Gay pilot—describes the horrors of that day. The implication is clear: when words fail, violence escalates.

*The Discovery of Language* (1994) is set in 1,000,000 BC. Women dig into the ground and uncover scattered letters—first an "A," then a "G," followed by "I" and "N"—until they piece together the word *VAGINA*. They point at each other's bodies and, for the first time, feel shame. One woman has her hands cut off for masturbating.

The History of The World – The Discovery of Language

Meanwhile, men dig and uncover letters forming *PENI*—but before they can complete the word, the "S" falls off a cliff and shatters. Years later, a blind man attempts to reconstruct the lost letter. Then, in a final ominous moment, a man sharpens an axe.

Mulloy suggests that before language, there was no shame in sex or the body. But once words arrived and labels were assigned, shame, repression, and violence soon followed.

"They're quite abstract," Mulloy admits. "They're not strictly historical moments, but moments where something changes in how people relate to each other. I thought it was a way of making a series, but I didn't think anyone would back it—who's going to put something like that on TV?"

Mulloy had plenty of ideas for future episodes.

> Oh yeah, I could have gone on forever—the Age of Reason, the invention of writing, the Roman Empire, Jesus Christ… there was plenty of potential. It feels like, with each series, I keep going further back in time, trying to get to the roots of whatever's happening in the present.

# *THE TEN COMMANDMENTS* (1994–1996)

Falling a wee bit short of the intended 133 episodes of *The History of The World*, Mulloy shifted gears and turned his attention to another ambitious subject: *The Ten Commandments.*

> I became really interested in making a series because *The Ten Commandments* gave me built-in subject matter. Each commandment was a starting point—'Honor thy father and thy mother,' 'Thou shalt not steal.' The question was: what's my angle on this? Working in a series format meant I didn't have to think about what my next film would be—it was already laid out for me. I thought, well, this would be my take on it. Animation lends itself to that kind of episodic format. It gives you a subject to explore, like *Cowboys* did for me.

Before we go on, let's take a quick dive into each of the ten films from the series.

## #1 Thou Shalt Not Adore False Gods

A man sits alone at home on a rainy day. Suddenly, two men break in, steal his belongings, and tie him up. Day after day, month after month, he remains bound.

Thou Shalt Not Adore False Gods

Thou Shalt Not Commit Blasphemy

One day, a bug lands on his nose. In frustration, he smashes his head into a piano. Realizing the sound could be a way to signal for help, he begins striking more notes, hoping to be heard and rescued.

A year passes. His piano skills have grown impressive.

Twenty years have passed. His ghost finally escapes his body and masterfully plays Mozart. As he approaches the pearly gates, people gather around, drawn to his music.

Then, one day, a hand from above reaches down—and punches the pianist.

The end.

At its core, the film seems to suggest that, despite Mozart's music giving the man purpose, he is ultimately punished for idolizing something other than God—the very same God who allowed him to be robbed and bound in the first place. It's a bleakly ironic, almost absurdist take on faith, devotion, and the arbitrary nature of divine judgment.

## #2 Thou Shalt Not Commit Blasphemy

Inside a church, parishioners worship. A man yawns. Above them, God also yawns—until an angel whispers something amusing in his ear. In response, he unleashes a violent storm upon the village.

Remember to Keep Holy the Sabbath Day

The yawning parishioner struggles to keep his home warm for his ailing wife. When he attempts to board up the windows, the wind shatters them. Desperate, he races to the church to pray for his loved one. Then, an idea strikes—he takes the church's steeple cross and uses it to patch his windows. His family is saved!

In return, he replaces the cross with a toy boat. Outraged, the villagers decide to burn him at the stake—until a drunken God urinates on the flames, inadvertently causing a flood. Fortunately, there's now a boat on top of the church, which the man uses to save himself and his family, while all the devoted parishioners perish because of god's stupidity and cruelty.

## #3 Remember to Keep Holy the Sabbath Day

In 1939, as World War II begins, strange lights are spotted above the small American town of Joesville. Zeke goes missing, only to return days later, insane and muttering about aliens stealing his brain. He's placed in an asylum. Over time, Zeke recovers his sanity and memory, recounting his encounter with alien beings called the Zogs. He needs to warn humanity that the Zogs plan to destroy the Earth. But how can he stop them? Oh, wait—it's Sunday, so the aliens can't attack because it's church day!

Anticipating the *Intolerance* trilogy (where we meet the Zogs again), Mulloy takes a pointed aim at the arrogance of Christians and Americans, though one could extend this critique to many nations and religions. These groups blindly assume that everyone, everywhere—even beings from another planet—follow the same codes and customs.

## #4 Honour Thy Father and Mother

Meet the Tucker family. They're rich. Mr. Tucker is always on his phone, busy making money. Mrs. Tucker prefers her pills. Meanwhile, Tucker Jr. sits alone, staring blankly at the television, surrounded by stuffed animals. They claim it's all for him.

When the county race is announced, the Tuckers beat and bully their son into competing. It does not go well.

Sometimes, it's best not to listen to dear old Mom and Dad—especially when they're abusive, status-obsessed psychos.

## #5 Thou Shalt Not Kill

A relentless drought is destroying Josh's crops. Then, at last, the rain comes—only for a bolt of lightning to strike his wife dead. Soon after, tragedy piles upon tragedy as his three children and dog perish.

Devastated, Josh takes his own life.

When he arrives at the pearly gates, he comes face to face with God—and doesn't hesitate to tell the deity exactly what he thinks of His decision-making.

What happens when tragedy relentlessly batters the human spirit? How is one supposed to endure? And if given the chance, what would you say to God? In an ending that would surely horrify Bible-boosters, Mulloy doesn't hold back.

## #6 Thou Shalt Not Commit Adultery

Capitalism has collapsed. NASA is in disarray. Astronauts Tex and Mary Lou are stranded in space, with no hope of returning to Earth anytime soon.

Trapped together, the two married astronauts grow to love and long for each other, but both refuse to commit the sin of adultery—even though neither has a happy marriage. Tex's wife was always unfaithful, while Mary Lou's husband, Roy, was abusive.

As the isolation and tension mount, both begin to experience disturbing dreams—dreams are so vivid that the line between dream and reality begins to blur.

Mulloy, here, critiques a society where true, genuine feelings must be suppressed in favor of unwavering adherence to a rigid code—one that offers no room for exceptions or understanding.

## #7 Thou Shalt Not Steal

Hank, a man from Mississippi, works at the town's main company, Cisco. He's an honest guy—so much so that even though he knows some of his co-workers are stealing from the company, he refuses to turn them in, even after failing to convince them to change their ways.

As the thefts accumulate and eventually contribute to the company's downfall, guess who benefits? Not Hank.

Once again, Mulloy delivers one of his sharpest and most timeless critiques. Despite everything we're taught about honesty, it doesn't always pay off. And just look around us: Musk, Trump, Putin, and nearly every oligarch or world leader. In reality, honesty rarely leads to freedom or success.

Thou Shalt Not Bear False Witness

## #8 Thou Shalt Not Bear False Witness

A man and woman both fail to meet their parents' expectations as children. In an attempt to appease them, they marry each other. The couple lives a loveless life, yet they put on a façade, pretending everything is perfect.

At night, they each have vivid, erotic homosexual dreams, but by morning, the dreams are forgotten and dismissed as mere fantasies. They continue their lives, playing the role of a perfect couple in the eyes of society, despite the truth of their false existence.

A tragic tale that has played out throughout human history, all because of inane and illogical moral codes. Thankfully, this tendency has shifted to some degree, though not enough.

## #9 Thou Shalt Not Covet Thy Neighbour's Goods

In a sort of sequel to *Thou Shalt Not Steal*, Cisco, after the collapse of his original company, relocates to Mexico, where he restarts his business under the name Cisco's Electrical Systems. There, he begins manufacturing torture devices, all the while thanking God daily for his wealth and fame.

But soon, the people begin to revolt. With poor pay and abysmal working conditions, tensions boil over. A worker is shot, and riots ensue. The army is called in, and the movement's leaders are arrested and executed using the company's very own devices. In the end, they descend to hell, but strangely it's still better than the lives they led.

Eventually, Cisco returns to the United States and runs for president—sound familiar?

## #10 Thou Shalt Not Covet Thy Neighbour's Wife

Finally, in what stands as one of the most bizarre episodes of the series, a man is so determined to win the love of his neighbour's wife that he switches places with her beloved dog (even trains the dog to walk and talk) so that he can win her adoration.

As with *Cowboys* and *Laughing Moon*, *The Ten Commandments* expose a system (in this case, religion) that fails to meet the complex needs of individuals and ultimately destroys them. Mulloy's characters live in a world

Thou Shalt Not Covet Thy Neigbour's Wife

defined by stifling polarity, one that doesn't align with their multifaceted, often contradictory desires and needs. Those who step outside the rigid framework of societal expectations are often ridiculed and denounced. In response, these "transgressors" take extreme, sometimes absurd measures to fulfill their needs while maintaining the illusion of normalcy.

Mulloy urges us to examine the impact of systems—like capitalism—on the human spirit. When we think of mental health issues today, we often focus on finding solutions through medication or therapy. But few ask if the true cause of our distress lies within the capitalist/consumer system we're all forced to exist within. When we struggle to function in this system, society asks, "What's wrong with you?" or "Why can't you be normal?" When will we step back and, as Gabor Maté has done in his book *The Myth of Normal*, ask deeper, more difficult questions about the root causes of our so-called mental or emotional problems?

We live in a society that constantly preaches empathy, compassion, and mindfulness—worthy traits, no doubt. Yet, we continue to elect or support leaders who embody the exact opposite qualities. The people who seem to succeed are the ones without empathy. "And people follow them—not everyone," Mulloy observes, "but enough people, like in America right now, to let them get away with it. In fact, they encourage it."

The idea for *The Ten Commandments* came not from external influences but from Mulloy's personal experiences. Raised in the Catholic Church, Mulloy recalls the hypocrisy he witnessed. "There was none of the love business—'Do unto others as you would have them do unto you.' They were aggressive and not very nice."

Humor played a significant role in shaping his films. No longer a believer in God, Mulloy found contradictions in many of the commandments, especially those concerning sex and stealing. "Wealthy people steal money and get away with it, while poor people get caught and thrown in jail," he noted.

His work often explores hypocrisy, particularly among those who publicly uphold religious or moral values. As we often see in daily life, it's the biggest Bible-thumpers who tend to commit the sins. How many times have we read stories about politicians who preach family values, only to be exposed for committing adultery, or those who are anti-LGBTQ, then get caught in a same-sex encounter?

*The Ten Commandments* series took between six months and a year to complete. Unlike some of his previous works, these films didn't air on Channel 4. "They just went to festivals. I didn't even send them to many. It's very hard to watch them all at once. I suppose I didn't make them for festivals. I made them for myself, to work through something. I'm never quite sure what, but it's something."

As with his other series, Mulloy worked quickly and instinctively on each episode. "I'd finish something, and by the next day, I'd be working on something else. It's like writing. The actual look is important, but not that important. I didn't want it to get in the way of doing." He contrasts his method with other film-makers who spend extensive time on design. "If somebody takes a long time to do something, I'll try to do the opposite."

This philosophy has driven him to explore new ideas. "I've always wanted to explore areas that are 'wrong'—the way things aren't usually done—because I think that's where you find something new."

Ultimately, *The Ten Commandments* is about good people trying to live a good life and do the right thing, but religion gets in the way. And surely, it's not supposed to be that way.

## *THE WIND OF CHANGES* (1996)

A departure from the minimalist, grotesque black-and-white worlds of Mulloy's previous works from the decade, *The Wind of Changes* combines his two passions—documentary and animation—to profile his occasional music collaborator, Alex Bălănescu. Bălănescu's throbbing, discordant soundtrack—unceasing throughout the film—creates a layer of tension while simultaneously mirroring the monotonous repetition of communist life. This score accompanies Mulloy's poetic and experimental portrait of Bălănescu's rise as a musician and the political challenges he faced, interwoven with his own recollections of key moments from his past.

Bălănescu's pulsating score, combined with Mulloy's black ink cut-out drawings—punctuated by dashes of red and blue, along with occasional archival images—creates an evocative piece that explores not only personal history but political history as well. References to the Soviet Union, shootings, and New York in 1978 intersect with Bălănescu's devotion to music, his sacrifices, and the pressures of childhood. More like a memoir than a traditional documentary, the film includes narration from Bălănescu, adding depth and reflection to the piece.

Despite its tonal differences from Mulloy's previous films—lacking satire or humor—*The Wind of Changes* remains true to his thematic concerns, ultimately exploring an individual's struggle within an oppressive communist system.

Bălănescu recalls endless tours, struggles with drugs and alcohol, the monotony of playing the same song, and a deep dissatisfaction with performing—likening it to being a parrot, trapped in a cycle. He remembers the sacrifices, the discipline, the constant pressure to succeed—it felt like a prison. There was no childhood, no time to play, only work and study. He was anonymous, stripped of personality. Individuals were not welcome in this system. These fragmented memories reflect life in communist Romania—marked by insecurity and fear.

"It was like a documentary, really, but I could blend a sort of poetic approach with it—make it slightly fragmented," recalls Mulloy. "I could take what he said about his life and use it to represent something. We sat down with a tape recorder. I asked him questions—'What happened after you left Juilliard?' 'Where are you now?'—and then we just cut it down to a 15-minute film."

Despite the film's unconventional approach, Bălănescu was fully on board. "He didn't say, 'Oh God, you've got someone shitting on someone's head, take that out.' He didn't care about that. Some people wouldn't have liked me taking the piss out of their serious business of producing music, but he went along with it."

One sequence was inspired by Bălănescu's mention of a girl he once saw on the street. "I don't even know if it really happened to him. I think it was a little girl he quite fancied. But it made a scene, and when you're doing something like that, you go with what someone remembers, because it obviously held significance for him."

The Wind of Changes

Beyond personal memories, the film also examines the political and societal forces that shaped Alex's worldview. "It was about trying to combine the politics of the moment he was living through—his relationships, how they formed his view of music. That idea that you can learn by rote, and how he always worked against that. I identified with that feeling."

Mulloy saw connections between *The Wind of Changes* and *Possession.*

> There are images in *Possession* of someone getting beaten with a hammer, and my daughter saying 'A, B, C, D.' I used that again in *The Wind of Changes*—the way the state forces conformity onto people. It's a different type of conformity than what I was dealing with in *Possession*, but it's still about demanding a certain way of working, a certain way of seeing things. That if you do it their way, you'll be successful.

The ending of *The Wind of Changes* is particularly striking. In the final scenes leading into the credits, Alex climbs onto a rocket, holds on, and soars into the sky. Then the screen begins to fragment—the images tear apart, the frame skitters, and then everything simply stops.

Mulloy managed to secure a bit of funding from the BBC for the film. "I try to find a way to make a bit of money. I knew the BBC was doing something, and I thought, 'I'm working with a composer—why not use that? Get the money to make a film.'"

Surprisingly, despite its layered complexity, *The Wind of Changes* wasn't scripted or storyboarded. "It was just based on words," Mulloy admits. "I was making it up as I went along. It was great, just making it up. You're not just sticking to a roadmap—you're allowing things to happen. Which is much more interesting."

The film also marked the amicable end of the collaborations between Bălănescu and Mulloy. While Mulloy admired Bălănescu's work on *Possession*, *Cowboys*, and *Sound of Music*, he found the process challenging.

> Alex did his own thing. He never showed it to me before it was finished. I'd just go to the studio, and with *The Sound of Music*, it was quite difficult because it wasn't what I expected. I had to grow to like it, and in the end, I thought it was fantastic. You have a kind of idea in your head, and I thought the music should have been a little closer to the way it was being played. But in the end, I thought it was great music.

By the time Mulloy began working on his *Intolerance* trilogy, he wanted more input into the music. "I wanted to sit next to the musician and discuss it with them. I kind of lost the Eastern European blues feel that Alex had, but it gave me other advantages."

## *THE CHAIN* (1997)

One of Mulloy's finest works explores how the systems we've inherited are rooted in ignorance, miscommunication, and greed. An indifferent parent discards a child's drawing. A street drunk picks it up, mistaking it for a treasure map. Soon, everyone wants the map, and world leaders rally their troops to claim the supposed treasure. The drunk digs furiously into the ground, but his people, fed up with his obsession, revolt and bury him. There is celebration, peace, and joy—until a hungover man stumbles across a piece of paper that looks like a treasure map… and the cycle begins again.

At once a ferocious denunciation of religious and political greed—and the mass killing carried out in the name of peace and love—*The Chain* rises above mere rant through its nuanced awareness of the complexities behind these systems. With strong Hegelian echoes, the final scene suggests that humanity will never learn from history, doomed to repeat the same costly mistakes.

Mulloy recalls: "I think it just began with a child doing something. I didn't know why I started that way or where it was going. I think I was making it up as I went along because I remember thinking, 'How the hell is this going to end?'"

Rather than opting for a dramatic resolution, he focused on the cyclical nature of human behavior. "It was about the cycle of things—how something

*The Chain*

happens and then repeats. It wasn't like anybody was defeated—it was just: this is how humans are. They will continue fucking each other up. It's not something that's ever going to be solved."

Colour became a significant part of the process this time. "I thought I'd introduce color into that," Mulloy explains. Unlike his previous black-and-white aesthetic, *The Chain* was an experiment in vibrant, almost chaotic hues. "It was like painting with your fingers," he says. "I've always had a problem with color, and my way of overcoming it is not caring," he admits. His approach was intuitive and unrefined. "I could sit here thinking, 'Does this go with that?' But instead, I just took the raw color—yellow, red, blue—and put it on. Used my fingers or whatever." This mindset freed him from traditional aesthetic constraints. "Making it look horrible was easier because then I wasn't trying to appeal to anybody."

Unsurprisingly, given the often inverted, hesitant, and conservative nature of the international animation community, *The Chain* received muted reactions. "Nobody came up when I showed *The Chain*. I thought, 'Oh, this is quite good. It's a story, it develops, what it's saying is strong.' But when I showed it—no response. Nothing."

Despite the lack of immediate response, the film's themes remain just as relevant today. "Watching what's going on in the U.S., as one example—it's still relevant," he muses. His films continue to stand as raw, unfiltered examinations of power, cycles of violence, and the structures that govern society.

## ***THE SEXLIFE OF A CHAIR* (1998)**

With *The Sexlife of a Chair*—a silly and hilarious collection of different sexual acts (masturbation, kissing, coitus interruptus, romance, voyeurism, sadism, bestiality, safe sex, etc.) involving, yes, chairs, all narrated in German to give it a pseudo-serious tone—Mulloy embraced an entirely different

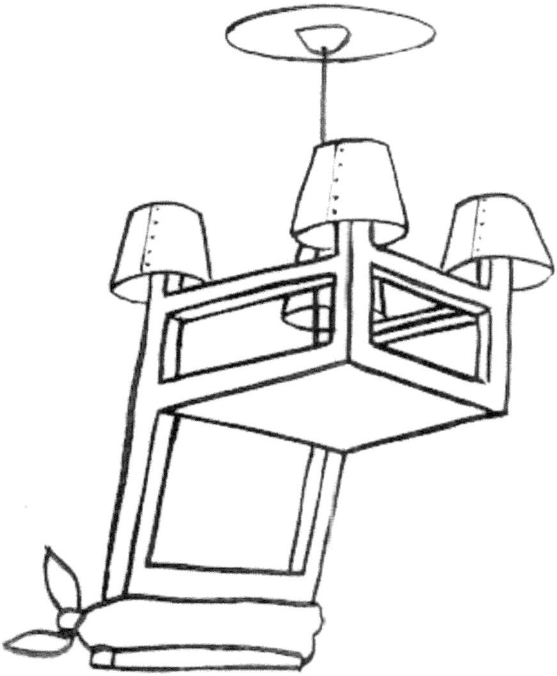

The Sexlife of a Chair

approach, one that would later evolve into *The Christies.* The concept was simple: do as little as possible and let the audience do the work.

"Put an image in their head with a title, and they'll create an image themselves," he explains. "If you have masturbation, you're going to have an image in your head somewhere."

This minimalist technique relied heavily on suggestion rather than explicit depiction. The pauses between texts allowed viewers to make their own connections. "That was what I became interested in," he says. "What's the minimum you can give the audience so they do the rest? They fill in the background, they imagine what's going on behind the scenes—because you never actually see it. That's where that idea began."

So, why chairs, you might ask? Well, it seems Mulloy has a bit of a fascination with these everyday objects. "I've used chairs a lot. It's one of my favorite objects," he notes. "I use them in *Possession*—a lot. I love the shape of chairs. To me, they've always represented a kind of logic—a mathematical logic. You sit on it. It works. If I can get a chair in something, I will."

When developing the visual structure of the film, Mulloy experimented with different ways of portraying intimacy using inanimate objects. "I can't remember the day I had the idea for *Sex Life of a Chair*," he admits. "But I must have thought, 'That's a good one.' You know how it is—you get some stupid thing in your head, and once it's there, you can't leave it alone."

The film's stark simplicity was further enhanced by its German voiceover. "It gives it this serious, educational-film feel," he says. The narration, however, subtly distorts over time, adding an eerie layer to the experience. "I was thinking of *Wavelength*. That idea of movement—of things developing, but still being a progression forward."

Music also played a crucial role in setting the tone. Mulloy turned to composer Peter Brewis for the film's atmospheric piano score. "I went round to Peter and just asked, 'Have you got any music? Can you do a piano piece?' And I thought—it was poetic. The logic of the chair. The poetry of the music."

Most film-makers probably would have gone with 1970s-style funk—something straight out of a sexploitation film from that era. But Mulloy, being the contrarian, went in a completely different direction. "I wanted something slightly romantic—just a kind of longing," he says. "But it works. Peter's good at that kind of thing."

*The Sexlife of a Chair* was entirely self-financed, giving Mulloy the freedom to explore his minimalist vision without external constraints. Looking back, the film marked an important turning point in his approach to film-making, setting the stage for future experiments in the 2000s—exploring just how little information a film needs to convey meaning.

Season's Greetings

# *SEASON'S GREETINGS* (2000)

Well, wouldn't you know it? Mulloy began the 21st century by once again taking a completely different aesthetic direction. In this greeting card for the new millennium, he blends computer animation with live-action footage to parody sentimental holiday greetings. It all starts off innocently enough, with a chorus accompanying a Dickensian-style illustration of a Christmas village. It's all so damn warm and cuddly... but we know it won't last.

And it doesn't.

The scene dissolves unexpectedly into an aquarium window, where a fish stares directly at the audience—text falling from its mouth—before a fist appears, knocking on the glass. A voice asks, "Is there anyone there?" The scene then shifts to a fish and chips shop near Bethlehem. Missiles fly overhead. A man in a helmet appears, staring blankly at the screen. The fist reappears, knocking on his helmet, repeating the question. What follows is a surreal collection of hybrid animals: a camel, an elephant playing with a ball, and the severed head of a donkey mounted on wooden wheels. In the film's final moments, we see a wreath dripping with blood before the same fist returns—this time knocking on the film screen itself. The voice repeats, "Is there anyone..." before abruptly cutting off.

It's an odd, ominous work—one that speaks to the anxieties of the era, from Y2K paranoia to the uncertainties of a new century. Looking back, *Season's Greetings* takes on new meaning in an era where the internet and the pandemic have heightened feelings of alienation and disconnection.

*Season's Greetings* was, in part, a response to those who accused Mulloy of repeating himself. "People write books with their hands. No one complains that it's the same hand," he quips. Still, the criticism pushed him to experiment.

> I come from an art background, and part of that is experimenting—finding different ways to represent things. Picasso had his Blue Period. Then Cubism. Then Neoclassicism. Some artists do one thing forever, but many move around—because creativity is about exploring ideas.

The film marked a new phase for Mulloy as he fully embraced digital tools. "I just wanted to see what worked and what didn't." These tools opened up new possibilities. "Suddenly, you could cut things out. You could put a lion's head on a chicken's body. That fish—I went to the London Zoo, saw this fish just staring out, and put letters coming out of its mouth. It was just nothing. But I was fascinated by the possibilities of computers."

The film's closing moment puzzled some viewers. "Oh yeah—the last shot is the blood. Then I thought, 'Oh, this is getting horrible again.' So I put something nice at the end. Like a Christmas card. *Season's Greetings*." The mix of bleakness and irony is a signature of his work. "I love the nasty undercurrent."

Another striking element is the recurring helmet imagery. "The guy in the helmet, someone knocking on it—it was about television forming a barrier between people. You can't see through the glass of the helmet." He recalls shooting additional material with a showerhead as a microphone, inspired by *Alphaville*. "That film really impressed me. Godard could just pick something up, talk into it, and it became a way of communicating. I was thinking about that when I was doing this."

Many of the film's moments arose spontaneously. "Sometimes you do something without knowing why, but then you reinforce it later. Like knocking on the television. I didn't plan that, but it created meaning. Meaning from nowhere." This open-ended approach allowed unexpected ideas to emerge. "Leaving things open—to see what you can create. Rather than sitting there planning everything out. That's how that film worked."

At the time, Mulloy was also learning how to integrate sound and visuals. "That was when I was trying to build an editing system—sound, visuals,

Love Is Strange

putting things together. Now you just need a laptop. Back then, it was hard. You can see how crude the images were. There was a relationship between the real image and the made-up image."

Despite his enthusiasm for the experiment, he never felt the need to revisit this particular style. "I enjoyed doing it. Didn't want to do any more of it, but I enjoyed it at the time."

At this point in the story, we are breaking free from the shackles of chronology so that we may devote the next chapter to Mulloy's trilogy, *Intolerance*, which was made before our last film of this wonderful chapter (it is wonderful, right? You're enjoying the conversational tone and casual insight into this master artist, right? Hello? Is there anyone. . oh never mind…let's move on and talk about love).

## *LOVE IS STRANGE* (2002)

In this twisted, bubblegum-colored surrealist tale, two magicians—Edward the Good and Eric the Bad—perform for the King and Queen, each wielding a magic pencil to impress their royal audience. Edward dazzles, while Eric… well, Eric is a bit of a disaster (to be fair, his bad Elvis impression didn't help).

Desperate to win favor, Eric resorts to drastic measures—he snatches the royal baby and makes a run for it. Edward gives chase. What follows is a frantic, *Harold and the Purple Crayon*-meets-*Simon in the Land of Chalk Drawings* showdown, as the two magicians use their enchanted pencils to outwit each other in a chaotic, *Tom and Jerry*-style pursuit.

But Eric soon learns that kidnapping a baby is no small feat—especially when said baby turns out to be a witch. Chaos ensues. In the end, Edward saves Eric, who, in an unexpected turn, kisses him as an act of gratitude (or maybe magic). The result? Eric transforms into a princess. Not a *beautiful* princess, exactly… but a princess nonetheless.

And so, in true fairy-tale fashion, they fall in love and live happily ever after.

*Love is Strange* marked another departure in Phil Mulloy's film-making, taking on the structure of a colorful fairy tale while maintaining his signature surrealism. The film was funded by S4C, a Welsh broadcaster, though Mulloy recalls the production environment as somewhat rigid. "It was a very kind of backward place," he says. Chris Grace, known for his Shakespeare adaptations, was involved in similar productions at the time. "They were awful. A lot of money went into those. And I just got a small amount to make this."

This time around, Mulloy worked with animators rather than creating everything himself. "It was good. Because the work wasn't that close to me. It was rough, which was fine. I wouldn't have wanted it to be too polished." He valued the collaborative process. "I like working with people. When I was doing live action film, I was always working with people—editing on location. But I was also used to sitting in a room alone, writing."

The script was loosely structured. "I think I wrote it. But I didn't do a storyboard. Maybe I did something very rough. But since it had a voiceover, I could just write the narration and illustrate it from there." Reflecting on the finished piece, he feels detached. "I'm glad I didn't animate it myself. I would have been totally bored with it. But when I look at it now, I think, 'Oh, that's okay. That's a nice ending, isn't it?' A film with a nice ending."

Admittedly, it's a minor film and one that Mulloy wasn't entirely comfortable with, to the degree that he didn't send it to festivals. That said, having Eric and Edward fall in love and having one 'transition' was, inadvertently, ahead of its time. And sure, it's not Mulloy set out to make a transgender love story, but at no point is that relationship considered anything but normal.

The intensity and rapid-fire madness of Mulloy's work defined what was a remarkable creative decade. "There was urgency in me. And I still feel it—I'm always trying to work as quickly as possible. Maybe it's some kind of autism, I don't know. I just want to get things done and out there."

Looking back, Mulloy reflects on how these films are remembered today:

> I haven't watched them in a long time. But yeah, I suppose they were the most energetic things I did in that period of my life. Ironically, I was actually quite calm back then, but the energy came from doing something I really enjoyed. I never thought, 'This is going to change the world.' Films don't work like that. But they can shift things a little—extend the vocabulary of animation. At the time, I remember thinking that animation was this tired little backwater of creation, stagnant. It was easy to go in there, stir things up, and splash around a bit.

## NOTES

1 The Clash, "Clampdown," on *London Calling*, Columbia Records, 1979.
2 Kitson, p. 144.
3 Kitson, pp. 145–146.
4 https://www.independent.co.uk/arts-entertainment/film-british-animation-ica-london-1586368.html

# Idiot Wind—The *Intolerance* Trilogy

# 3

The new century saw Mulloy diversifying in terms of style, technique, and format. The most impressive of these works is the *Intolerance* trilogy and the assorted features and episodes about the Christie's family (we will meet the Christie's in Chapter 4).

Before we hear what Mulloy has to say about the *Intolerance* trilogy and dive a bit deeper into the films, let's quickly go through each film for those readers who have not seen the films (which is inexcusable since they are readily available on YouTube). In fact, this is a perfect spot for you readers to pause so that you can go watch the trilogy. It'll take you about an hour. Okay, go, I'll wait here and keep the page warm.

## *INTOLERANCE* (2000)

A voice jokes, "Ready when you are, Meester Dee Mile," acknowledging we're watching a film (and a nod to Billy Wilder's 1950s jab at Hollywood, *Sunset Boulevard*).

On a spaceship, scientists find a mysterious film canister in space debris. Years later, one deciphers its reversed label—ZOGFILM. They play it, revealing a documentary about the planet Zog, where inhabitants are literal dickheads, with faces as sex organs and vice versa. The footage, broadcast across Earth, shocks audiences as it depicts Zog customs: shaving their dickheads, kissing resembling intercourse, and babies feeding through straw-like mouths.


DOI: 10.1201/9781003527909-3

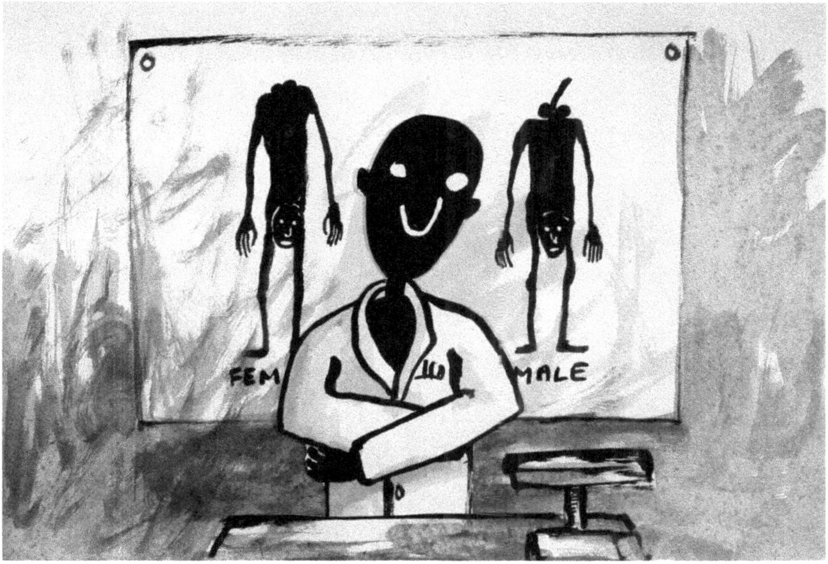


Intolerance

Reactions range from horror to outrage. A religious viewer demands the film be stopped over graphic imagery, while another scene hilariously reveals that handshaking is taboo, yet thieves are idolized like oligarchs. Despite their grotesque habits, Zogs believe they are made in God's image—just like humans. One similarity? They get drunk and watch TV on Christmas.

As the film continues, Earth's audience grows enraged, demanding an attack on Zog. Meanwhile, the Zogs, having seen a similar documentary about humans, prepare to destroy Earth.

## *INTOLERANCE II: THE INVASION* (2001)

The human and Zog fleets are on a collision course, each intent on destroying the other. But when they finally meet after ten years, distractions—an Earth pilot sniffing his girlfriend's panties and Zogs watching porn—cause them to pass by obliviously.

The Zogs prepare for their invasion by learning to act human, cutting off their heads as disguises since their faces double as sex organs. They land conspicuously on Earth during the Olympic Games and blend in.

Intolerance II

Thirty years later, at Ma Tucker's, KKK member Dwight Hokum drunkenly discovers the hooded racists are actually Zogs. When no one believes him, he starts shooting indiscriminately and later creates The Church of the Solitary Believer, gaining influence. A devoted viewer, Hanna, falls in love with him, and they marry, maintaining an unusual sex life that satirizes religious conservatives. When Dwight uncovers a shocking truth about Hanna, he takes violent action.

Meanwhile, the Earth fleet continues toward Zog.

## *INTOLERANCE III: THE FINAL SOLUTION* (2004)

After 2,000 years in space, Earth's battle fleet has found nothing. Factions have formed—especially the Anti-Zog group, who doubt Zog exists (and think Elvis is alive). A police captain yells "SHIT!" when their leader escapes—only for an officer to take it literally, squatting mid-defecation.

Intolerance III

Aboard the ship, grotesque body artists provide entertainment. Meanwhile, police officer Abe's girlfriend, Eva, doesn't believe in Zogs—causing tension. The Archbishop, oddly wearing panties on his head, is consulted about the fugitive. To conserve space, people over 40 are recycled into burger meat.

The pro-Zog leader devises a plan: transform body artists into fake Zogs, film them, and fool Earth. "People believe anything they see," a line eerily predicting A'I's role in misinformation. This raises a question—was the infamous *ZOGFILM* human-made all along?

Captured Anti-Zoggers suffer the worst torture—endless Disney movies. In a bizarre twist, only Elvis can save humanity, mocking celebrity worship.

Finally, Abe and Eva (yes, that Abe and Eva) reach Zog, discovering a lush paradise. But where are the Zogs? Alone except for an apple tree, they face a biblical parallel. In the mildly happy ending, a distorted nod to *Thou Shalt Not Commit Adultery* suggests that art itself is the last hope.

With echoes of *The Chain*, *Intolerance* comically and savagely explores the cyclical stupidity of humanity. Humans end up killing each other over a fear of a race that never even existed! (Yes, that's a spoiler—but I told you to watch the films, didn't I?)

It's no coincidence that the epigraph "Mirror, Mirror on the wall." opens *Intolerance.* The trilogy and certainly most of Mulloy's films grab a mirror and jam it in our faces, forcing us to ask some awkward questions about our society, beliefs, and choices. The fact that Mulloy's films regularly polarize audiences is apt… the very people offended by the 'zog's' habits in

Intolerance II

*Intolerance mirror* those in Mulloy's audience who are offended by his blunt depictions of the society's hypocrisies and, well, idiocies.

In some ways, the *Intolerance* trilogy (the title is a nod to the 1916 silent film epic by the racially problematic director, D.W. Griffith) acts as a compendium of earlier works like *Cowboys*, *Ten Commandments*, *Laughing Moon*, and *The Chain*, as Mulloy dives head (or dick?) first into racism, xenophobia, nationalism, misinformation, cult of celebrity, gender, and sexuality—with his signature sharp edge.

Mulloy masterfully shifts between crude humor—packed with dick and sex jokes—and a biting critique of society. He delivers a prescient take on how easily we are divided along the lines of sexuality, gender, and national identity, exposing the absurdity of these manufactured divisions. "Divide and conquer," as the saying goes, and Mulloy captures this perfectly—the way fear and prejudice fuel new forms of hatred. In this case, intolerance toward a race that, ironically, was human all along.

Although Mulloy could not have foreseen the extent to which misinformation would evolve—or fully grasp the broader negative implications of technology and the internet on society—the revelation that the *Zog* documentary is, in fact, fake makes *Intolerance* a prescient work, eerily relevant to the complexities of the modern world. Even before the internet, discerning truth from falsehood was a challenge.

Though Mulloy claims this wasn't on his mind when creating the films, it's worth noting that *Intolerance* was made in the wake of 9/11—at a time when the U.S. government, with the backing of a compliant media, manufactured claims that Iraq possessed nuclear weapons to justify its invasion.

Media, Hollywood, and politicians have long manipulated reality. However, since the advent of the internet—and more recently, artificial intelligence (AI)—this distortion has escalated exponentially.

AI has now reached a level of sophistication where people are routinely deceived by fabricated images and articles. Reports of foreign interference in national elections are becoming more frequent—Russia is regularly accused of orchestrating misinformation campaigns, and India was recently alleged to have played a role in electing a conservative hardliner in Canada.

We are drowning in an endless flood of images and information, bombarded from every direction. How can we possibly combat it? How do we distinguish truth from deception? Perhaps the only solution is to disconnect—to shut it all off and focus on our own immediate realities.

Before I arrived in Lviv, Ukraine (where I am writing the bulk of this book), my mind was clouded with misconceptions about what life would be like in a war zone. In fact, before we travel anywhere, we are often influenced by speculation and assumptions—most of which turn out to be baseless, shaped by media distortions or the singular, subjective experiences of others. Maybe the solution is to only trust what you experience, to concentrate on your lot of experience in the world, and to carve out the best possible choices or experiences? But maybe that's a load of hogwash. As Mulloy's work has suggested, none of us are angels; we all have darkness within, so maybe we are in the world we deserve? Or are those inner inclinations manufactured by the prevailing systems we are raised within?

Mulloy didn't initially conceive of *Intolerance* as a fake documentary when he began working on the film. "I just started drawing, and the idea came as I was working through it. I don't plan things out too much. I work quite intuitively. I just trust myself in terms of where I'm going."

Fake news isn't Mulloy's only target in *Intolerance*. The film also takes aim at the inherent artificiality of cinema—particularly science fiction films and documentaries. Influenced by the over-the-top cheesiness of old Hollywood sci-fi, Mulloy playfully critiques the medium itself. At the same time, the film's central conceit—a fake documentary that sets the entire plot in motion—subtly underscores the dangers of cinema and television. Regardless of genre, both have a profound, often unconscious impact on how we perceive the world, shaping our views on love, family, and war.

Consider how many Hollywood films glamorize war or how documentaries, often taken as objective truth, can be deeply manipulative—what's left out of the frame is often as telling as what's included. Cinema has also

Intolerance III

reinforced narrow, one-dimensional portrayals of other cultures. How many Hollywood films cast foreigners as villains? Yet, we rarely question these narratives, often surrendering critical thought the moment we enter the theater.

Mulloy's films frequently critique and parody American culture, yet they also carry an element of admiration. "Of course," Mulloy acknowledged.

> I was brought up on American films. As a child, you'd go to the cinema a couple of times a week. When an English film came on, it just didn't have the excitement, the energy of American films. It looked very provincial. I didn't think in those terms then, but intuitively, you felt it—the titling, everything was just more mundane. So yeah, it was the American films I liked.

His perspective shifted when he attended film school and discovered world cinema.

> I stopped liking or watching American films when I realized there was a whole load of other films being made in other countries. As interesting as American films were, others had their own language, their own way of organizing films, and they weren't bound by the same rules. You'd read these books about the 'rules' of cinema and narrative, and then you'd see people like Godard and think—wow, this is something else. The freedom to construct a new way of understanding film.

Mulloy also acknowledged how American cinema shapes perceptions of culture, both within and beyond its borders. "Cinema defines who people are. The Americans have done that—not just for themselves but for others. Many of our ideas about America and other cultures were planted in us by film."

Reflecting on contemporary American society, he saw parallels between conspiracy-driven movements and cinematic narratives. "A lot of what's happening in America today—QAnon, people suspicious of the FBI—it's the films they've been watching," he observed.

Mulloy's portrayal of characters often leans toward absurdity, something he hadn't consciously analyzed. His familiar stick figures serve as funhouse mirrors reflecting hollow people—no depth, no refinement, no room for middle ground. It's an either/or world, occupied by hollow-eyed dickheads. Everybody in these films are just twits. "I don't sit down and write films about dumb characters. But yeah, I suppose they are about the stupidity of people," admits Mulloy.

His critique, however, is primarily aimed at systems rather than individuals. "People go along with the rules set for them," he said.

> Especially in *The Ten Commandments*, or even *The Sound of Music*—that's just about how society is organized. And you can see it getting worse. A few people at the top, and then the oligarchy growing in America. But *Intolerance*? Yeah, it's just idiots. They're going across America in *Intolerance 3*.

The side story of an Elvis cult, as absurd as it may seem on the surface, aligns perfectly with *Intolerance*'s broader themes of misinformation and blind belief. Through Elvis, Mulloy not only satirizes a culture that elevates celebrities to godlike status—treating their words as unquestionable truth—but also nods to the accusations of cultural appropriation that surrounded him.

*Intolerance III* – Elvis Lives

Elvis built his persona on a style and sound heavily influenced by Black artists, often without acknowledgment.

Beyond that, his death itself became a breeding ground for conspiracy theories. After he died, rumors spread that his death had been staged, leading to years of alleged Elvis sightings.

Elvis entered the *Intolerance* series almost spontaneously. "I was going to make the film in a studio in Germany, and I thought it might be a nice idea to use Elvis in the script so I could have a German Elvis impersonator sing one of his songs," Mulloy explained. The chosen song, *Wooden Heart*—based on an old German folk tune—is performed at a wildly inappropriate moment in the film, adding to the absurdity. Mulloy found humor in the idea. "There was a period when people claimed to have seen him at California's Legoland amusement park, and all sorts of places. And people really believed it. Sometimes, people want to believe things so much."

This cultural myth fascinated Mulloy, providing an opportunity to incorporate music and transform Elvis into a quasi-religious figure. "I thought I could put some music in here, and Elvis could become like a god. They call him 'The Elvis,' don't they?" he said. "Every city has an Elvis person. It also fits with this whole mentality of idolizing figures like Trump," he added. "He's got the same haircut as Trump—a nice quiff, an old quiff."

Beyond conspiracies and celebrity cults, Mulloy revels in the absurd and unpredictable. "When you're doing a film, especially in animation, you can be as crazy as you want," he said. "You don't want people to know what's coming. I try to make a story that's followable, but I also like to have unexpected elements. Making Elvis the head of the Zogs—why not?"

Hope is hard to find in *Intolerance*—or in any of Mulloy's films, for that matter—but if there's any glimmer of it, it comes from art. The film's ending presents a world that is, quite literally, unified, as the body artists merge into one. It's a darkly poetic resolution to a story that spends so much time dissecting division.

But hold up—Mulloy quickly dismisses that grandiose interpretation. "Not really. It was silly, really. They were destroying themselves to create something." He explained that body modification and tattoo culture were becoming more prominent at the time, and he simply incorporated those elements into the film. "It didn't come into my head out of nowhere," he said. "Things generally arrive because they're around you." While the imagery suggests themes of connection and unity, he insists he wasn't advocating for any grand solution. "No, it's ridiculous," he said with a laugh. "But it's an idea of connection—of people working together rather than apart."

Of course, Mulloy primarily wants us to laugh—and we do—but it's an uneasy kind of laughter, the same kind we experience when watching Trump, Musk, or the assorted buffoons in power. Like the best comedians, he forces us to laugh at the things we wish weren't true. In that sense, Mulloy is the animation equivalent of Bill Burr, Andy Kaufman—who created grotesque characters like Tony Clifton and his wrestling persona to both feed and mock America's appetite for violence—or George Carlin, using comedy to expose society's absurdity and cruelty. He doesn't offer solutions—only a mirror and a sly smirk.

Mulloy understands that humor is essential to his satire, often grounding his sharpest critiques in personal anecdotes. "The one about him kissing his great-aunt," he recalled, "I just remember when I had a great-aunt, and if you looked at her face—people at that time had their faces covered in powder. And they stank of some kind of lavender or something. Christmas was always a bit of an ordeal, having to kiss them." These small, absurd details add a layer of familiarity to the film's broader critique, keeping it from becoming too heavy-handed. In the end, Mulloy isn't just exposing society's absurdities—he's inviting us to laugh at them, even as we recognize the unsettling truths beneath the punchlines. What the hell else can one do?

The roots of *Intolerance* go back to 1997 or 1998, around the time Mulloy was making *The Sex Life of a Chair*. He stopped working on it, feeling it was just going to be the same territory as earlier films. When he returned to it, he just dove in without any outside funding. "I just started doing it," he explained. "I tried to get money for it, and nobody was interested. So I just started making it." He worked on the film for about eight months before securing funding from various sources, including Channel 4, the Lottery Fund, and the London Production Fund. "That's why it's easier to work if you can control it yourself," he said. "If somebody offers me some money, I won't take it."

Initially there was no thought of a trilogy or anything beyond a single film, but by the end of the film, Mulloy realized that there might be more to the story. "When I got towards the end they were so angry, they were going to go out and invade the Zogs, and wipe them out," he said. "So yeah, I thought, yeah, I left it open. I thought, the name *Intolerance I*—it's got that kind of grandiose idea behind it. And it needed episode 1 somehow. A ten-minute *Intolerance* was not big enough."

The success of the first film allowed him to leverage funding for the sequels. "Channel 4 gave me the money for the next one," he noted. "Number two was Channel 4, Film Council, and Canal+ Spain. I must have approached them. I can't remember now, but I vaguely can. I wrote to them and asked if they were interested. I think they came in quite late."

With *Intolerance II: The Invasion*, Mulloy shifted towards digital tools while also incorporating colour. "At one time, I had a Steenbeck, all the old stuff," he recalled. "But things were just getting a bit easier. You were starting to get computers that you could edit on. So you could edit the sound on it as well, and it made the actual production quicker." The first *Intolerance* film was likely created on 35mm film, while the second incorporated digital techniques. "The second one, I don't think I filmed it," he said. "I can't remember. I don't think I put it on 35mm. The first one was 35mm. The second one had color, and I was actually colorizing it on the computer. I was making it on TVPaint—it was called Aura then. It's one of those apps I've been using for the last 20 years."

For *Intolerance III*, Mulloy worked with the acclaimed Stuttgart-based studio, Film Bilder. It was a good match and one that made sense given that one of the key figures at the German studio was animator, Andreas Hykade, whose style and tone shared similar sensibilities with Mulloy.

Thomas Meyer-Herrmann, head of Studio Film Bilder, also recalls that the experience was positive for both Mulloy and the studio:

> Gabriele Roethemeyer, head of our regional funding MFG, brought us together. Phil had told her about his project *The Final Solution* – I assume it was at the Stuttgart Festival of Animated Film in 2002. Gabriele Roethemeyer suggested an English/German co-production to Phil and recommended us. I already knew Phil, also from the festival, and thought it was a wonderful idea. The project was then financed by MFG, Studio Film Bilder and Phil himself. It was animated at Studio Film Bilder based on Phil's storyboard, his design and direction – four months with four animators. I think it was Phil's first personal project with a team. It was also a challenge for us because of the (for us) unusually long running time of 24 minutes, with a modest budget. This was possible thanks to Phil's not only ingenious but also efficient way of working and a relatively new animation technique at the time: digital cutout. Phil prepared the individual shots in Photoshop, and the animators animated them using the Cel Action software. It was phenomenal to me how much freedom Phil gave the animators and how much the result was still clearly a film by Phil Mulloy. It also fit well with the other two films in the *Intolerance* trilogy, even though Phil had made them single-handedly. After this positive experience, Phil and I wanted to tackle a feature film project next: *Mirrorland*. Unfortunately, we didn't manage to get the financing.[1]

"It was really good." recalled Mulloy.

> I had storyboarded that quite closely since they needed direction. I was in London, they were in Stuttgart, so I couldn't be there often. But they were proficient. They tried to make the movement look like mine, but their animation was much better than what I could do for that kind of thing.

The studio's small team of about four people worked closely with Mulloy's material. "I actually produced something for them to work from. My characters were basically like the cowboys I usually draw, just in different costumes. They understood that, and it was great."

While Film Bilder's animators didn't influence the story, they contributed within scenes.

Intolerance II

> They would offer ideas in animation, trying to humanize the movements. Sometimes I'd go with it, sometimes not. My characters don't really look human, but their approach was interesting. I'm open to that kind of collaboration. If something works, I'll use it—even if I initially said I wouldn't. You may as well use the animators' creativity too.

Mayer-Hermann recalls how unique the experience was working with Mulloy:

> Phil Mulloy is known as a one-man band, as a prototype of the auteur who does everything alone. That's why it was so surprising to me how well he was able to work with a team. He got the animators to implement his vision without exerting any pressure. I found these 'stage directions' in the file lake. They are certainly not complete with respect to the entire film, but they show how few instructions Phil needed to give. Among Film Bilder directors, there are others who manage with hardly less than 20 comments per shot. Animation people can be control freaks. Phil is the opposite – and still gets pretty much exactly what he wants.[2]

Here's a snippet of the "stage directions":
Hendrik

1. shot 141 more police
2. shot 209a bring in trooper crowds one after the other
3. shot 50 put crown on the leader
4. shot 55 hold archbishop head looking up at dreaming heads after he speaks—make the two followers of the archbishop bow down at front of shot and then hols them still
5. shot 59 get rid of bounces of background

6. shot 23b put troopers in chasing followers
7. shot 25 make zoom in on ade faster.
8. shot 107 take hip hop dancer right off screen right. Ie. make shot longer.

Ralph

1. shot 60—cake up in one movement—not up and then down
2. shot 80a use psd I sent you for sympathizers
3. shot 78 loose window cleaner—hold end longer ade closes his eyes
4. increase flashing intensity in torture scene
5. shot 181 pause a liitle before ade speaks
6. shot 77 make lem sobbing last longer
7. shot 106 reduce size of body artists—keep consistent with others
8. shot 120a put in extra shot of CU starting of player (psd sent).

Following the completion of *Intolerance,* Mayer-Hermann and Mulloy considered making an animated feature film, *Mirrorland*, but couldn't solicit the necessary funding. "You've got to jump through so many hoops." The abandoned project centered around a satirical take on Father Christmas, reimagining him as a capitalist tycoon with oil fields. However, the process of pitching was frustrating. "I'm useless at presenting things. You have to stand there and convince people to give you money, and I'm the last person who can do that. They want to see something they recognize, but I don't even know what it is."

Past attempts to work with producers had also left him disillusioned.

> I fell out with one producer—it was a nightmare. Since I started working the way I do, any attempt at a feature has not been pleasant. If someone asks me if they should do a feature, I tell them no. If there's money in it, you're stuck. You're not free to play around, because someone is always telling you what won't work.

Following the *Intolerance* trilogy and an abandoned feature project, Phil Mulloy created a few short films that hinted at the stylistic and narrative directions he would later pursue in *The Christies* and acclaimed shorts like *Endgame.*

Mulloy notes that *Intolerance III* was the last time he was "really paid for a film." While this was undoubtedly frustrating for an established and award-winning artist, it also granted him creative freedom. The advent of digital tools allowed him to experiment with new styles and storytelling approaches without financial constraints.

*On the Coastline* (2006) is an oddity, with its closest comparison being the computer-tinged *Season's Greetings*. The film consists of three photographs:

On the Coastline

the first, a portrait of Jean Julius Sibelius by Yousuf Karsh; the second, an image of a Roman soldier sculpture; and the third, a childhood photo of a five-year-old Mulloy. Using lip-sync animation with computer-generated voices, each photograph becomes a character in the film.

In the first segment, "Sibelius," the composer, as if in a therapy session, speaks to an unseen person about winds, rain, a woman, and a coastline. In the second segment, the Roman soldier reflects on walking along a seawall, the "utter futility of life," and an intimate experience. Finally, in the third segment, a young boy (with a sped up and distorted voice by Mulloy) recounts to an unseen man how a friend abandoned him. He describes a surreal scene of men near a cliff, dancing and roaring like tigers.

Mulloy admits that *On the Coastline* is a strange piece.

> I don't know why I made it. I had this book of photographs by Yousuf Karsh—the prints are incredible. There's a portrait of Sibelius that I found amazing—he looks like a beast or a clown. I became fascinated with heads, with faces. It was just a simple animation trick—quick and easy. It doesn't quite work, but it was like a forerunner to AI-generated imagery. You could see where things were headed.

More importantly, *On the Coastline* also anticipates the flat minimalism and computer-generated voices of *The Christies* films.

*Brockwell Park* (2007) is a minimalist work—even for Mulloy—a surrealist slice of life unfolding over the course of a day in a park. A raw, white stick-figure man takes his dog for a walk. Along the way, a plane flies overhead, a car passes by, and another driver vomits out of his window. The man briefly notices a woman in passing.

Once at the park, he plays fetch with his dog. Each time the dog chases the ball, it embarks on surreal adventures—conversing with a fish, playing with a woman. Mulloy employs stark black-and-white contrasts, with the dog colliding against a black frame. As the man and woman become increasingly engrossed in the game, their mutual attraction becomes evident. Meanwhile, the dog accidentally leaps into the water and is rescued by the same fish, now holding balloons that float it back to the surface.

Later, the dog enters an igloo-like structure, as if leaping through time and space, freed from the constraints of physics. The playfulness ends when a larger dog appears and takes the ball. The solemn man and his dog return home, where a drawer full of identical balls awaits them.

Mulloy created *Brockwell Park* using NewTek Aura, an early 2D paint and digital software package that later evolved into TVPaint. "It was just a fun little piece," he recalls.

> I'm sure there was some meaning behind it, but maybe I won't go into that. It was more about seeing how little you could use to create something.
>
> I actually made it before *The Christies*—I was searching for ways to create something small-scale without making it feel large. *Brockwell Park* was along those lines—trying to find something from almost nothing.

While *Brockwell Park* might appear scripted, Mulloy insists that all of his work follows a spontaneous process.

> Even with *Intolerance*, I had no idea where it was heading—I just knew it was about people being shocked by others' behavior. What some see as normal might be outrageous to someone else. It all comes down to agreed social boundaries—what's acceptable and what isn't. I didn't know *The Zogs* would end with them attacking that place. I didn't know the next one would follow from that. The only time I had to plan more was for *Intolerance III* because I worked with a studio. I didn't have to—I was happy to. It was great.

Despite the assumption that digital tools would allow for greater improvisation and cost savings, Mulloy found the transition challenging at first. "Digital tools weren't as fluid then as they are now, so in some ways, working on paper was easier for me."

Nevertheless, it is both surprising and refreshing to see an artist embracing digital tools so readily. "If something comes along that I can do something with, and I think, 'Oh, that's interesting,' then I use it." This adaptability aligns with Mulloy's minimalist and unpretentious philosophy from the start. "I'm not aiming for perfection. I'm not trying to frame a stunning sunset or anything like that. I just do it and say, 'That's it.' I don't over-design. I don't make mistakes—I just know what I'm doing when I do it."

Despite his reluctance to make features, Mulloy would next embark on a series of strikingly original animation features that stand among his finest and most polarizing achievements, *The Christies*.

## NOTES

1 Email exchange with the author, March 31, 2025.
2 Email exchange with the author, March 31, 2025.

# Meet the Christies

# 4

*"A family's like a gun; you point it in the wrong direction and you're gonna kill somebody."*[1]

*Forgive me—or don't. I don't really care, because you're not here right now. I'm typing this from a dentist's office in Western Ukraine. I'm breaking the so-called fourth wall between writer and reader because, well, because I can. I'm now thinking back to the first time Phil Mulloy sent me (via the Ottawa International Animation Festival) a DVD containing a bizarre bunch of animated shorts about a family named the Christies.*

*This was the mid-2000s, a time when animation—particularly animated features—was still dominated by safe, saccharine stories churned out of Hollywood boardrooms. Phil hadn't intended these shorts to be seen as a single film, but after watching them all, I suggested (at least that's how I remember it and he doesn't dispute it) he splice them together into a makeshift feature. Did I think it was a masterwork? Honestly, I wasn't sure. But as someone with a soft spot for chaos and a mild instinct to stir shit up, I found this jagged, lo-fi "shadow puppet" anti-family sitcom with deadpan computer-generated voices—and a character named Mr. Hitler—refreshing, to say the least.*

*It was weird. It was bleak. It was funny. And unlike so much animation then and now – it definitely wasn't precious.*

*Ottawa audiences are pretty tolerant—used to having strange, uncomfortable films thrown at them—so I figured a few folks might appreciate the satire and experimental narrative. But I also knew it would be polarizing. When the jury announced that* The Christies *had won the Grand Prize for Best Feature, I was pleasantly shocked. When the next two Christie's films* Goodbye Mister Christie *and* The Pain and the Pity *also won the Grand Prize in subsequent years—with entirely different juries—it was nothing short of astonishing. And it gave me a flicker of hope for an art form that too often plays it safe.*

*Alright, back to our story.*

Oh wait, before moving on, let's note another oddity in the Mulloy canon: *Flik Flak* (2001). I know this breaks chronological order—Phil only


DOI: 10.1201/9781003527909-4

sent me a copy during the late stages of writing this book—but it's worth a brief detour. *Flik Flak* is an unusual collaboration between Mulloy and fellow UK animation legend, the late Paul Bush. "Phil and I are friends and we admire each other's work," recalled Bush in 2005. "There was a 5 part three minute slot available on Channel 4, and we decided to start from scratch (putting aside our own particular specialities) and try and devise a series for it. We wrote them together and I animated one, Phil the other."[2] Only 2 three-minute episodes were made.

This digital short is a candy-colored, sci-fi-tinged piece featuring geometric characters who spout nonsense in computer-simulated voices. It centers on a father, mother, and son, and one can't help but sense the germ of the Christie's family emerging from this flickering, bizarro tableau of semi-characters adrift on a digital screen.

"I remember Paul and I would meet just because we were friends," recalled Mulloy.

> Paul was good fun, and so the experience of working with him became that also. It turned out that the short film that we produced looked like nothing we would never produce alone, but I know that some of the images and thoughts I brought to *The Christies*, became a major influence on my own work some years later.

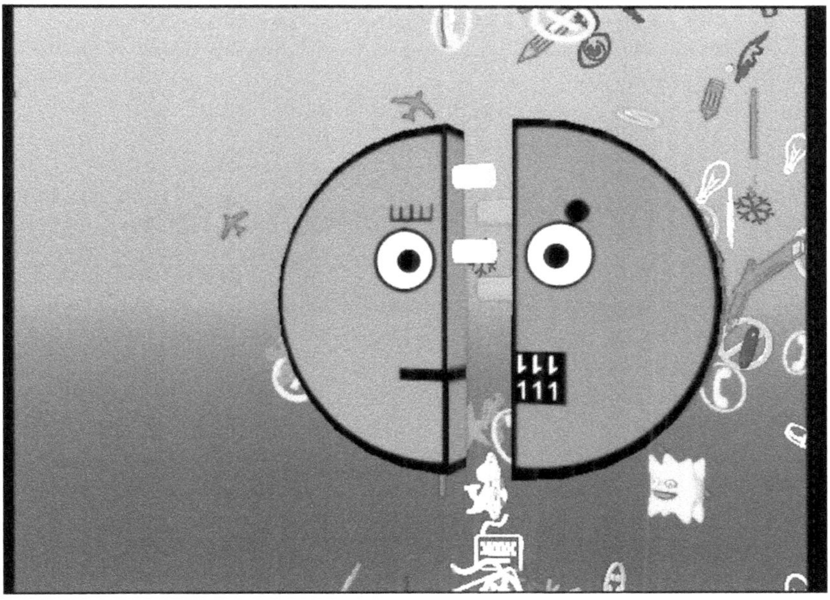

*Flik Flak*

Alright, now let's meet the Christies. This highly dysfunctional family would appear in several features and shorts: ***The Christies*** (2006) – the aforementioned stitched-together feature comprised of 11 BBC shorts produced in 2005, ***Goodbye Mister Christie*** (2008), ***The Pain and the Pity*** (2010), and ***Dead But Not Buried*** (2013). In 2013, a half-dozen Channel 4 shorts followed, along with a few stragglers: the unreleased ***Catastrophe*** (2014), ***That Sound*** (2015), along with a handful of mini-episodes ridiculing Donald Trump and Boris Johnson.

## THE CENTRAL CAST

- **Mr. Christie**: Our bitter, miserable antihero—a man convinced that everyone exists solely to torment him.
- **Mrs. Christie**: His long-suffering wife, who harbors secrets of her own.
- **Terry**: Their softly defiant son, obsessed with rockabilly star Gary Challenger.
- **Tracey**: Terry's girlfriend, who frequently tries to control Terry, while rarely concealing her dislike of his parents.
- **Buster**: Their "talking" dog. He only barks but some claim to understand him.

## SUPPORTING CHARACTERS

- **Mr. Yakamoto**: Mysterious Japanese man who might not be who he seems
- **Mr. Hitler** (yes, really)
- **Tina**: Terry's older lover initially but who appears later as a TV show host
- **Father Bunloaf**: The unstable priest who is hot for Mrs. Christie
- **Uncle Tony**: Mr. Christie's brother
- **Ramon**: Mrs. Christie's therapist-turned-lover

Together, they form the twisted, darkly comic universe of the Christies—one of Mulloy's most audacious creations.

The Christies

The visual style? Think shadow puppetry meets Rorschach blots—faces as anonymous black blobs punctuated by crude geometric features. No expressions. No realism. Just silhouettes and suggestion.

*The Christies* (2006) is a pitch-black, chaotic, and absurdist portrait of a deeply dysfunctional family. It's a disturbing ride through absurd moral dilemmas, bizarre social commentary, and relentless critique of Western society's hypocrisies, all wrapped in minimalist animation and deadpan computer-generated voices. The film's disjointed nature reflects the fractured lives of the Christies, whose petty desires, frustrations, and existential crises collide in increasingly surreal ways.

The film opens with Mr. Christie, a bitter antihero, being interrogated by a faceless authority figure. His sarcastic responses and absurd, often self-destructive behavior set the tone for what follows—a world where rationality breaks down, and chaos reigns. The film's fragmented structure—the product of originally separate shorts—mirrors the disarray of the Christie family, each segment offering a twisted slice of their dysfunctional lives.

In *Family Values*, the Christies' son, Terry, is obsessed with kneeling and refuses to stand, while his father, Mr. Christie, is drunk and belligerent. The absurdity escalates when the family's odd social issues—like Terry's desire to marry a woman named Tracey—become a public spectacle, with protesters chanting, "Everyone has the right to be on their knees!" This chapter sets the stage for the film's black humor, where absurdity is used to skewer generational divides and societal expectations.

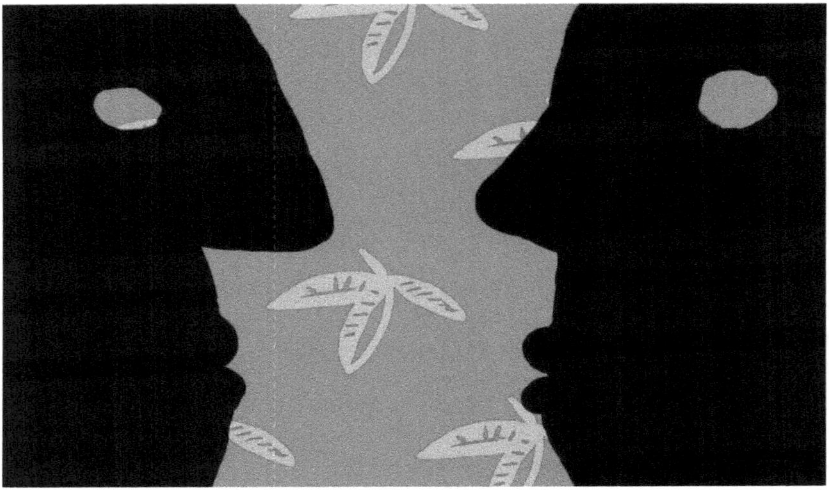

Family Values

*The Language of Love* dives into the twisted dynamics of Mr. and Mrs. Christie's marriage. As Mr. Christie proclaims that the meaning of life is death, Terry, meanwhile, falls for an older woman, Tina, and confides in their talking dog, Buster. This chapter showcases Mulloy's ability to blend surrealism with a sharp critique of impotence—both literal and metaphorical—highlighted by a comically impotent drawing of a penis.

Things take a darker turn in *The House Painter*, where the Christies hire a German painter named Mr. Hitler. His swastika murals and disturbing obsession with Tina make for a grotesque satire of racism and fascism, with Mr. Christie's bigoted reactions heightening the tension.

In *Tracey's Dream*, the narrative slips into dream logic, where violence and hallucinations take center stage. The scene's creeping dread and twisted visuals signal the film's capacity for both dark humor and unsettling moments of psychological collapse.

*A Song for Buster* marks a strange musical interlude, as dialogue loops and turns rhythmic, turning even the characters' voices into an unsettlingly absurd chorus. This surreal moment plays with the form of animation, turning it into a meta-commentary on its own absurdity.

In *The Confession*, Mrs. Christie admits to summoning the devil at work and cursing her husband. The consequences of this admission are as grotesque as the rest of the film, with Mr. Christie's head morphing into a freakish object, followed by a shocking self-inflicted stabbing.

*Natural Disaster* explores the absurdity of modern celebrity and self-worth through Terry's supposed "miracle" powers. As a dandruff storm

A Song for Buster

envelops the family, the Christies are caught in a surreal battle for control over Terry's newfound "healing" abilities—highlighting the absurd commodification of even the most meaningless phenomena.

The family's breakdown continues in *Mister Yakamoto*, as suspicions arise that Terry isn't Mr. Christie's biological son. This leads to a mix of bizarre, disconnected events, including an appearance by Mr. Yakamoto, a mysterious blues singer who may or may not be a pedophile, adding further to the film's deep sense of disillusionment.

*Gary Challenger* deepens Terry's descent into idol worship as he seeks a doll of his rockabilly hero, Gary Challenger, in exchange for leaving the family. Mr. Christie's own mental deterioration becomes more pronounced when he fixates on a duck no one else can see—representing his growing delusions and inability to control his environment.

*Mr. Christie's Sex Manual* is a warped commentary on sexual alienation and narcissism. In this chapter, Mr. Christie's inability to connect with his wife is depicted as an absurd sexual fantasy where he makes love to various characters and finally himself, underscoring his self-absorption and emotional isolation.

Finally, in *The Day the Earth Moved*, a strange, oddly beautiful chapter, the Christies are caught in a surreal encounter with a UFO. Mr. Christie's existential crisis reaches its peak as he is confronted with a peaceful alien who tells him that the universe knows him as "a small-minded piece of shit." The alien's message doesn't break Mr. Christie—he can't change, even when given the chance for love.

Mr. Yakamoto

As a collection of shorts, *The Christies* feels slightly more disjointed than the later *Christies* films. The audience is thrown directly into the middle of this chaotic family, and due to the flat, minimalist character designs, it can often be hard to tell who's who. While the computer-generated voices are subtly altered to give each character a unique identity, the differences remain minimal. All of this unfolds within a confined space—reminiscent of a live children's puppet show. The dialogue is nearly nonstop (something I normally abhor in animation films), but it's so strange and funny that you (or at least I) just roll with it. There's a lot happening quickly in this claustrophobic setting, and the viewer is really forced to engage and visualize. This isn't a series you can simply sit back and watch passively.

Obviously, this is not your average animated family. *The Christies*' blend of disdain, regret, lust, and deception is more honest than any sitcom. They may loathe one another, but they also resist society's expectations. Mr. Christie is a narcissistic monster—but everyone else exists solely to torment him. And, in a way, he kind of deserves it.

*The Christies* is an unhinged, layered, laugh-out-loud descent into animated madness. But it's also bracingly real. It critiques racism, masculinity, conformity, sexuality, and the modern family with such scathing absurdity that viewers either buckle in for the ride—or walk out. Either way, Mulloy is laughing, because we're all a bit like Mr. Christie: haunted by our parents, our impulses, and our inability to change or find stability, even when surrounded by family, friends, music, and love.

## *GOODBYE MISTER CHRISTIE* (2008)

Mr. Christie

The sequel opens with déjà vu. A narrator recycles the ominous line from *The Christies*: "Everything we are about to see is based upon reality..." It's Mulloy's way of telling us we're back in the same world—so don't get comfortable. If the first film was a fragmented portrait of modern dysfunction, *Goodbye Mister Christie* is its logical—and far more cohesive—meltdown.

We begin with a sunset and seduction. Ramon, a smooth-talking French sailor, oozes charm and innuendo as he flirts with Mrs. Christie. Soon, they're having sex. Soon after that, she confesses every detail to Father Bunloaf who gets so aroused he forgets his vows. Mr. Christie eventually joins in too—equally confused and curious. And from there, the film escalates: more confessions, more piercings, more TV cameras, and an increasingly frenzied collapse of any remaining order.

Mulloy again uses his signature minimalist animation—flat, expressionless characters drifting across color-blocked backdrops. But this time, the aesthetic feels sharper, more deliberate. The visual sparseness becomes a part

Ramon

of the satire: when the background vanishes entirely, the characters themselves start to question it.

Compared to its predecessor, *Goodbye Mister Christie* flows with a strange sense of narrative momentum. The film's chapters—each with their own absurd premise—start to interlock. As the Christies spiral into chaos, the film tightens its grip thematically. Mulloy is still riffing on sexuality, repression, and family dysfunction, but now he's also blasting fame, ego, digital culture, media voyeurism, and the hypocrisy of both institutional power and the counterculture.

Terry and Tracy, once rebellious avatars, now embody the shallowness of modern dissent. They pierce themselves not out of conviction but out of boredom and a craving for attention. When Terry is arrested for a murder he didn't commit, he confesses just to impress Tracy. When that fails, they try becoming porn stars. Eventually, they too meet Ramon. You can guess what happens next.

Meanwhile, Mr. Christie becomes world-famous for having sex on live television. He's declared a prophet. Mr. Yakamoto compares him to Christ. Buster the talking dog grows resentful. Father Bunloaf grows mad with lust and guilt. Mr. Christie digs holes. And holes. And more holes. Until he exits the world entirely.

At a certain point, the film ditches realism altogether and dives headfirst into allegory and myth. Mr. Christie enters a white void. He meets his dead parents. Julius Caesar is there. Jesus. Hitler. A typically belligerent Mr. Christie can't understand a word he says.

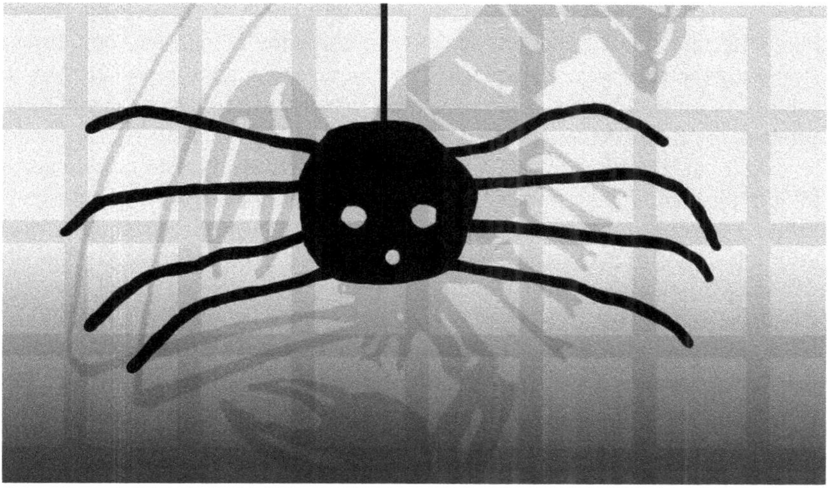

Spider God

These surreal encounters evoke films like Pasolini's *Teorema*, where an outsider's erotic influence destabilizes a household, or *A Christmas Carol*, where the protagonist becomes an unwilling witness to their own moral unraveling. Father Bunloaf confesses his desire for Mrs. Christie, which eventually leads to his blinding—a gruesome nod to *Oedipus Rex*. And as the universe begins to dissolve, Mulloy even mimics *Intolerance*'s climactic ending: images flicker, characters morph, voices overlap. It's as though cinema itself is collapsing.

When Mr. Christie kills God—who has taken the form of a spider—the film becomes overtly philosophical. Without a deity, there can be no order, no afterlife. The camera and blood are all that remain, poised to become the foundation for whatever world comes next. Or doesn't.

For all its sexual surrealism and deadpan humor, *Goodbye Mister Christie* is ultimately a more focused film than *The Christies*. It's still anarchic, but now that chaos carries a purpose.

"I began thinking about the film as a complete fantasy in which Mr Christie was trying to escape from something awful that had happened to him," adds Mulloy.

> Something that was so bad that it would drive him to extremes. When I was a child, we had a small garden or rather a patch of dirt behind the house. I often wondered that if I kept digging and digging down through this patch of dirt, would I finally reach Australia. This fantasy became the main structure on which the film was based.

Mulloy targets not just the nuclear family or the church, but something larger: our collective thirst for attention, our performance of outrage, our obsession with spectacle over substance. The characters gradually realize they're trapped in a cheap production, imprisoned by narrative tropes, by visual minimalism, by their own scripted stupidity.

And yet, the film doesn't wallow. It laughs. Even the end credits are a joke: hundreds of fake names and roles scroll by, parodying the industry's inflated self-importance. In reality, it's the work of one man, using a skeletal animation style to dismantle everything from God to Google.

As Mulloy's world collapses into a white void, only two things survive: the blood and the lens.

***Dead But Not Buried* (2010)**, billed as a sequel to *Goodbye Mister Christie*, continues the bleak, absurd, and often disturbing journey of the Christie family. This film returns to the mysterious fate of Mr. Christie, who was seemingly trapped underground in the previous installment. The film opens with a search for his body, but as the search is called off, the story quickly shifts into new layers of intrigue and bizarre events.

The mysterious birds from the previous film make a return, discussing rain in Wellington Green, and Mr. Yakamoto's obsession with bringing Mr. Christie back to life becomes a central plot point. As the film unfolds, we follow a series of increasingly surreal developments, including Mr. Christie's body being transported to Iceland, where Mr. Yakamoto believes he can reactivate his brain. Alongside him is Tina, who remains skeptical but is forced to contend with the oddities around her, including her boss's dangerous fixation on Mr. Christie and her near-death experience at the hands of sharks.

The characters are driven by their own selfish motives—Ursula, Mr. Christie's wife, still grappling with guilt and affairs, and Terry, now more consumed by his own desires, all while the Christies' world grows more absurd and hostile. Mrs. Christie confesses her infidelity to Father Bunloaf and reflects on the fallout of her actions. Meanwhile, Tina's search for vengeance against Yakamoto grows more intense after her horrific encounter with sharks leaves her mutilated, setting the stage for a climactic confrontation.

The plot dives deeper into conspiracies surrounding Mr. Christie's Tesco sticker collection, as various characters claim familial ties to him, including a bizarre parade of apparent siblings vying for their share of his legacy. The lines between reality and delusion blur, with Mr. Yakamoto's failed past as a cartoonist and potential Russian spy becoming central to the mystery. His relationship with Miss Okobe, who is growing increasingly frustrated with his behavior, evolves as their twisted dynamic mirrors the absurdity of their quest to reanimate Mr. Christie.

Mulloy's minimalist animation, combined with his sharp critique of capitalist and consumerist ideologies, creates a dissonant backdrop to the family

Tina in Hospital

chaos. The vibrant colors that marked the earlier films are replaced with a grayish wash, emphasizing the emotional and moral desolation that pervades the Christies' lives.

The tension escalates as the characters converge in Iceland, each with their own agenda: Yakamoto continues to work on his experiment to bring Mr. Christie back to life, while the Christies and the "siblings" search for the coveted Tesco sticker collection. The fractured nature of their relationships and selfish pursuits leads to a series of increasingly violent encounters, culminating in a climactic scene where everyone, even those claiming to seek peace and love, turns on each other in a chaotic shootout.

Ultimately, the film delves into a broader existential despair. The characters' fixation on materialism and self-preservation proves stronger than any desire for love, redemption, or change. Mulloy's cynical view of humanity, especially within the context of the film's claustrophobic environments, makes it clear that, despite any pretensions of spiritual or emotional transformation, these characters are hopelessly entrenched in their flaws. Even the title *Dead But Not Buried* feels like a cruel joke, as the characters struggle to break free from their self-imposed prisons, unable or unwilling to change.

In the end, the volcano erupts as the film concludes with a twist of dark irony: Mr. Christie, though reanimated, is not the savior he had hoped to be, and the world remains as fractured and doomed as before. Mulloy's bleak message resonates even more in 2025, as the film's scathing commentary on selfishness, materialism, and the inability to change feels painfully relevant. The Christies may never change, and neither, perhaps, will we.

# *THE PAIN AND THE PITY* (2013)

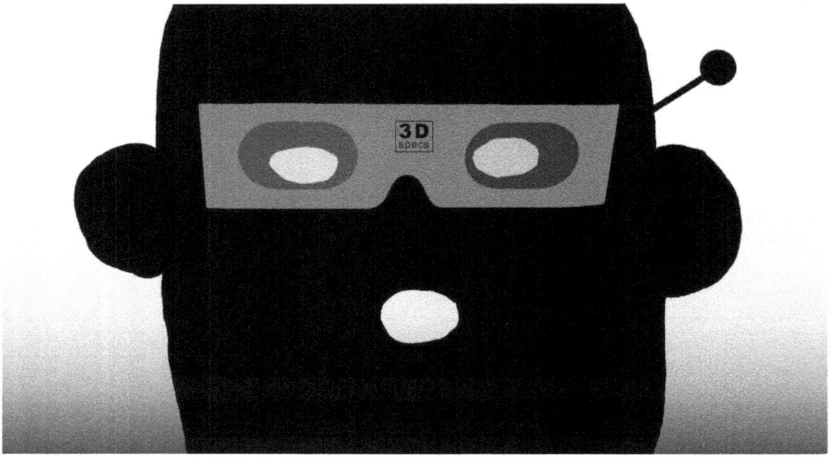


Andy

The final Christies' film opens in smoke and whispers—fragments of beginnings and endings colliding. It repeats the same narrated text as the earlier films, now spoken in a barely audible voice, as if dissolving before it even begins. Credits roll not at the end but at the start—again. Familiar names scroll over the volcanic smoke, the very image that closed *Dead But Not Buried*. Mulloy loops time back on itself, stitching his films together with a kind of cinematic déjà vu.

The characters, now overexposed against a white void, seem to know they are in a film. They complain about being unemployed, uncredited, forgotten. "Mrs. Christie" is furious—three films were promised. They speak not just in character, but as actors, as people. Or something close to people. No one has ever seen the director. They were hired by letter. They begin to feel a chill, a ghost of uncertainty.

Terry searches for Phil Mulloy online and finds a photograph of him as a five-year-old boy. The whispering voice returns, heard only by Roger (the actor who played Father Bunloaf). The spider god reappears, briefly, ominously. The characters resolve to contact their creator. It all echoes Pirandello's *Six Characters in Search of an Author*, but here they are not seeking to *enter* a play—they're trying to escape it.

The button appears. "Do Not Press." It gets pressed, again and again.

Walls shift. Music distorts. Red letters flash like corrupted subtitles. The characters are adrift in a space that may be a film set, a holding cell, or a metaphysical glitch. They begin to refer to one another by their real names. Roger can't find the exit. None of them can. It's a loop without a script. *The Exterminating Angel* recast with animations and flies.

"Yakamoto" dreams of birds and oil pipelines under Soho. His bird companion speaks the truth he tries to deny: he is lonely, forgotten, yearning. The narrative splinters into interior dialogues and shared hallucinations. Everything becomes porous—reality, performance, past, present.

The spider tells Roger he's the chosen one. He offers wealth, influence. But only if blood is spilled.

Is this the voice of the director? Or of something older?

Another actor, Ray, is found dead. A murder mystery unfurls, channeling Agatha Christie—but half-heartedly, like a performance from memory. The characters accuse each other, lose trust, eat less, speak more. History intrudes—photos of bombed cities, disappearing villages, distant wars. These images don't just appear; they *haunt*. The past flickers in like found footage from a forgotten reel. A voice says, "Nothing remains the same. Nothing." But nothing really disappears either. It just changes form.

Mulloy seems to be reflecting not just on the Christies but on cinema itself—its ghostly nature, its obsession with time and memory, and its—and our—inability to let the past rest.

Tadashi (Mr. Yakamoto) finally finds Heather (Ms. Okobe), the lost love he spoke of to the bird. Their reunion is tender but fractured by years and distance. He explains the beating he suffered, the hospital, the failed search. She waited, but life went on. They are not lovers anymore, just survivors of a story they never got to finish.

More deaths. The fly returns. Unkillable. He reminds them they are not people—only digital drawings and synthetic voices. Even that feels cruel.

Andy (who played Terry) wears 3D glasses and sees things differently. Red words appear through him. Roger becomes more desperate. Anthony (Mr. Christie) collapses under his own contradictions. The button is pressed again and again. Roger finally kills him.

Then, an opening. A whisper: "Look at the sky."

In the final movement, jittery footage of a man and a boy walking through Soho. Mulloy's voice tells us the date and time: May 2013, 8:30 PM. No one notices them. The city goes on. Red letters appear: "This is real."

Then: Mill Lane, Wallasey, 1863. A photo of a village that no longer exists. Another red text: "This no longer exists."

Roger becomes the richest man in the world. The boy disappears.

The credits roll—exactly as they began, just like *Dead But Not Buried*. A perfect circle.

Village

But this final film is more than an ending. It's Mulloy's meditation on memory, loss, and cinema itself. The characters, like all of us, are stamped by history. They try to escape their past, but the past persists—just beyond the frame, just behind the smoke. Their lives were never fully their own. They are voices conjured by a creator who remains offscreen. Maybe even haunted by his own memories.

Even in their simulated world, they ask the same questions we do: Who wrote this? Why are we here? And is there still time to change the ending?

# CHANNEL 4 SHORTS (2013)

*Goodbye, Mr. Christie* was intended as the last appearance of the character, but Mulloy says that he "enjoyed the process of making it so much that I decided to make another and another."

And so he did.

Around the time Mulloy was finishing the features, he also made another collection of shorts for Channel 4 about the Christie family. These are quicker, looser, and somehow more disturbing and hilarious than ever—like fever dreams that go from surreal to bleak to absurd and back again, usually in under five minutes.

Mrs. Christie

## LITTLE TERRY'S DREAM

Mr. Christie has a dream: he's a two-headed monster, Mrs. Christie is a beautiful princess, and Terry isn't in it at all. Terry seems hurt by that, so he shares his own dream. In his version, he's a superhero with a dog's body and a squeaky helium voice. He shoots his dream-dad dead, makes Mrs. Christie into an ugly old witch, and dreams about having sex with Tracy (but wakes up just before anything happens). Then Mrs. Christie has her dream: Mr. Christie is again a monster, Terry is a handsome prince… who also gets killed. There's this constant dream/revenge cycle happening, as if the family can only communicate through symbolic violence.

## THE SEX SLAVE OF TUNBRIDGE WELLS

Possibly the darkest of the bunch. Mrs. Christie interviews Mr. Christie, who stutters his way through a fragmented memory of being abducted at age 12 by a man in a black car. He remembers the smell of the upholstery, being slapped by the man—possibly Mr. Haines, the bank manager—and being taken to a small room where he was kept and abused. The details are unclear. The memory skips, glitches, and falls apart mid-sentence, like the film itself is trying to suppress or censor it. We only catch flashes: the room, the smell, the name "Marilyn." It's never spelled out completely, but it doesn't need to be. The horror is in what's implied, and how that trauma still seems to be leaking through him, decades later.

## STRAWBERRY CHEESECAKE

Mrs. Christie is making cheesecake because Sir Jumblesworthy is coming over. Mr. Christie starts coughing. Terry, of course, loves her cheesecake. Meanwhile, Buster the dog won't stop barking. They tell Mr. Christie his cough sounds like barking, which is probably why Buster's agitated. Then Tracy announces she can translate Buster's barks—and apparently, Buster thinks Mr. Christie is a fool, a bully, and just generally unpleasant to look at. Mr. Christie is outraged at what Buster "said," but maybe Tracy's just making it all up to mess with him. Then again, that somehow doesn't make it feel any less true.

## TERRY'S DEPARTURE

This one's mostly the family trying to sing. Terry and Tracy refuse. Mr. Christie forces Terry to join in. Then Buster wants in. Sir Jumblesworthy, too. It's all just guttural nonsense—everyone making strange noises and morphing into weird, inky Rorschach-like shapes. Terry's had enough. He's tired and announces that Gary Challenger is the best singer and leaves.

It's one of those rare moments where Mr. Christie seems to be genuinely trying to bring the family together—almost sweet, in his own aggressive, bullying way. Mrs. Christie is oddly moved by his singing and his clumsy compliments on her voice. For a brief second, the family actually feels like a family. Just barely. Almost.

## THE BANKER

Things get stranger. Mr. Christie is now wearing a Mayan mask and won't explain why. Turns out he's joined a Mayan end-of-the-world cult, invited

Buster

by Sir Jumblesworthy. The rest of the family is jealous. Terry is impressed. Mrs. Christie tries on a mask—even though it's a men's-only club. Terry and Tracy make their own.

It quickly spirals into a cycle of swearing and name-calling. It only ends when Buster attacks a stick figure from a Men's Only bathroom sign and bites off its penis… or maybe it was Mr. Christie? As Buster holds the severed penis in his mouth, an unseen voice whispers that it's not the end of the world—it could be a new beginning.

Strangely, there's no banker here. Unless the whispering voice at the end *is* the banker. Or maybe this is all a callback to Mr. Christie's earlier memory about being assaulted by a bank manager? Either way, it's classic Mulloy—where no horror is too deep to be twisted into a gag, and no gag too ridiculous to be haunted by something darker.

## BACKWARD FORWARD

Terry starts speaking backward. Mr. Christie is instantly annoyed and berates him, of course. Mrs. Christie jumps in to defend him, as usual, and starts translating his strange backward phrases. Eventually, Mr. and Mrs. Christie are both speaking backward, too. Terry says it's about learning compassion—for people who speak other languages, for those who sound different. It's a moment that almost, almost makes sense.

And then, out of nowhere, Terry asks: "Dad, why don't you ever tell me that you love me?"

The screen fades to black. The film ends. Just like that. A gut punch that slices through all the surreal comedy and grotesque noise. Even in reverse, it always comes back to the same aching questions.

Father Bunloaf

## *CATASTROPHE* (2014)

Mr. Christie proudly announces that this year's village Christmas play will be a Samuel Beckett piece. Terry is outraged—he wanted to play baby Jesus in a proper nativity. Mrs. Christie, meanwhile, recalls seeing a Beckett play once and finding it so painfully dull she had to flee the theater and vomit.

As the family spirals into rehearsal chaos, Mulloy uses the premise to brilliantly mock the pretensions of high culture, religious hypocrisy, and the hollowness of tradition. Mr. Christie's choice of Beckett—a writer of existential dread and silence—for a Christmas play becomes the perfect vehicle to expose his arrogance and delusion.

Terry, in a subplot of comic paranoia, discovers he's part Irish. He panics, fearing Tracy must never find out because, of course, she hates the Irish. This sets off a running thread of bigotry, as various characters casually spew xenophobia toward the Irish, people from Kent, Yorkshire, beggars—anyone perceived as "other." It's all absurd, and all delivered in deadpan, revealing the rottenness behind polite society.

Father Bunloaf arrives and announces he's leaving the Church—he's becoming a Muslim fundamentalist. His reasoning is vague, almost opportunistic, and his character becomes a darkly comic critique of religious institutions and their fluid, often self-serving allegiances. He also recounts a disturbing memory: getting spanked by nuns in front of the class and becoming aroused.

Terry, always desperate for love and attention, declares that his "dingle dongle goes hard" when his mother kisses him. It's shocking, but typical of Mulloy's world, where taboos are relentlessly pushed, often to reveal the sickness hiding beneath domestic and religious facades.

Tracy appears wearing a black sheet over her head. Father Bunloaf is aroused again. Mulloy leans into the surreal and perverse, satirizing both the fetishization of religious modesty and the grotesque sexual dysfunctions hiding within the family and church alike.

Mrs. Christie has a moment of quiet revelation. She now likes Beckett, she says, because he reduces everything to nearly nothing—and that's how she feels. "I don't know where I end and someone else begins," she admits. It's a rare moment of existential clarity and one of the few displays of genuine emotion. It also feels like a meta-commentary—Mrs. Christie becomes aware she's just a character in someone else's play, a puppet in Mulloy's bleak comedy.

Then, as if summoned by all this misery, Mr. Hitler shows up—claiming to be collecting for an army of street cleaners. But he's really there to drop truth bombs: Tracy, who rages against Kent, was actually born there. She kills herself. Then, Mr. Hitler reveals they were all born in Kent. Even Mr. Christie. It's a final punchline that collapses the entire web of snobbery and self-denial: the thing they all claim to hate is the thing they are.

The play ends. Abruptly. The screen fades to overly elaborate, faux-"prestigious" credits—Mulloy's last jab at artistic pretension.

*Catastrophe* is a savage satire of highbrow theater, organized religion, sexual repression, class snobbery, and the contradictions of nationalism—all under the guise of a family Christmas play. Every character is a bundle of hypocrisy. Every joke is a knife.

## *THAT SOUND* (2015)

A short but potent reunion with Mr. Christie. There's this strange, groaning sound—deep, unsettling. Mr. Christie hears it and starts obsessing over it. What is it? Where's it coming from? Is it real or just in his head? Is he going insane?

In the background, explosions flicker—digitally rendered blasts that seem to anticipate the more elaborate visual chaos of *Endgame* and *Once Upon a Time on Earth*. Are they signs of some distant catastrophe? Or just a fleeting visualization of Mr. Christie's own internal collapse? Probably both.

## TRUMP & BORIS MEETS THE CHRISTIES

In 2019, Mulloy took a jab at both Donald Trump and Boris Johnson in a series of online shorts, some of which included appearances from the Christies.

## HERR TRUMP GOES BACK TO WHERE HE CAME FROM

In this 30-second critique, Trump, Mr. Christie, and Mr. Hitler have an absurd conversation about flies and mosquitoes. Trump and Hitler both share a mutual hatred for them, but Hitler has an extreme solution: take babies away from their mothers and lock them in cages. The scene quickly dissolves into

The Christie's poster

haunting images of immigrant children in cages, a sharp and uncomfortable critique of Trump's policies that inadvertently draws disturbing comparisons to Nazi Germany.

## DID YOU HAVE SEX WITH BORIS?

Terry asks the bombshell question that cuts through all the chaos: "Did you ever sleep with Boris Johnson?" Without hesitation, Mr. Christie confirms that yes, his wife did. Terry then goes a step further, asking if she would sleep with Donald Trump. Mrs. Christie's response is quick and harsh: "Sleep with a rapist? No thank you." But then Mr. Christie, ever the opportunist, wonders if she'd reconsider if the U.S. offered a good trade deal.

It's a bizarre blend of dark humor and absurdity, but it also feels incredibly timely given the political dysfunction and trade wars dominating the headlines. The dialogue is both funny and deeply uncomfortable, forcing us to reflect on how far we're willing to go for power and economic gain.

## TRUMP'S DOG

Terry asks Mr. Christie who the man is walking a dog in the distance. Mr. Christie responds that it's Donald Trump, but the "dog" he's walking is actually Boris Johnson. Terry, confused, says it must be a woman since the person walking the dog has breasts. Mr. Christie, irritated, calls Terry stupid, insisting it's Trump, and moments later, Trump's wig blows off. Terry realizes his mistake. As they watch, Terry sees Trump seemingly hitting Boris, but Mr. Christie brushes it off, claiming Trump is just negotiating a new trade deal.

## AND NOTHING BUT

Terry, ever the curious one, wonders about something hanging off Boris Johnson's trousers—the "pink thing" between his legs. Mr. Christie immediately gets upset, telling Terry to shut up and reminding him that this man is our Prime Minister. But it's hard to ignore the absurdity of the moment: Terry is essentially calling Boris Johnson a "dick," both figuratively and literally. It's a crude, sharp jab that fits right into the Christies' world of chaotic, often uncomfortable humor.

–

*The Christies* stands as a stark, satirical exploration of the absurdities of family dynamics, societal conventions, and the darker undercurrents of everyday life. The series was never meant to be a traditional family comedy but rather a subversion of it. The Christies represent a family that's anything but idealized; they're messy, unrefined, and frequently ridiculous. Their interactions serve as a backdrop for Mulloy's critique of high culture, religious hypocrisy, political absurdities, and societal prejudices.

In an interview with the London International Animation Festival in 2011, Mulloy recalled:

> I became interested in computer- generated voices around 2000 and, in fact, made two shorts with the animator Paul Bush using the voices. They were really quite primitive and robotic. A couple of years later, I went back to the internet to see if the voices had progressed. They had. Now they were almost human. I began playing around writing dialogues, made a six-minute film, and became interested in the family.[3]

"Finding his voice was like finding a goldmine," recalled Mulloy.

> Wow! Someone had invented a real bastard of a middle-class Englishman. What was he invented for? Who could possibly want to use his voice but me? And then I found Mrs. Christie's voice. She, of course, was the exact opposite of Mr. Christie—gentle, kind, and accommodating. How, I thought, could she voice her resentments against such a tyrant?

Mulloy adds that Mr. Hitler was meant to be "like the guy next door, the neighbour who might pop in for a chat. He seems a reasonable, helpful chap, but Mr. Christie gets angry because he cannot understand Mr. Hitler's heavily German-accented English."

The other oddity, Gary Challenger, was not based on anyone in particular. "He just happens to be a bit of a pop star who decides he wants to help Terry be a singer," adds Mulloy. "Pop stars are very influential on children's behaviour, and Gary is no different. His methods of training are unusual, but many a pop star undertakes the rigours of his training."

Mr. Christie's voice, an essential feature of the series, is an embodiment of the show's satirical spirit. His pompous, pretentious tone, and xenophobia and his refusal to ever consider alternative perspectives make him an ideal target for Mulloy's sharp wit. He is the very definition of self-important ignorance, and his interactions with Mrs. Christie, who possesses a meek and

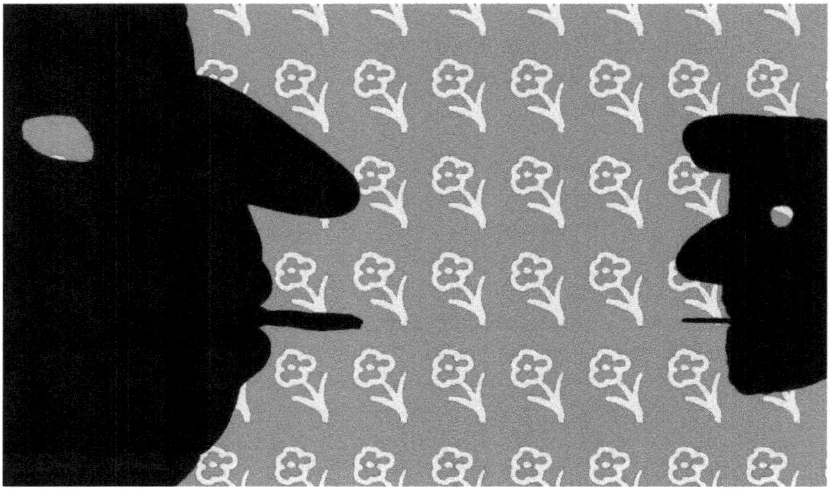

Gary Challenger

almost invisible voice, serve as a perfect foil to his arrogance. The contrast between them highlights the absurdity of the family's dynamics.

Mulloy experimented with simplifying character design, ultimately deciding to change just the shape of the mouth to create expression. "I thought, let's go as extreme as possible. Make it as simple as possible and just use the camera." He developed creative ways to depict interactions—panning shots and dynamic compositions—while keeping the animation style minimal. "That opened up a whole world for me on how I could, with very simple means, represent something quite complex. At the same time, I didn't want to give people too much—I wanted to leave spaces they could fill in themselves."

The first *Christies* short he made was *Little Terry*, which set the tone for the series. "Mr. Christie was telling Terry to get off his knees, but in a way, it was about people like Mr. Christie putting people on their knees," Mulloy explained. The children in the series exhibited an unsettling maturity. "They seemed to know a lot about sex, a lot more than they should. They were cheeky to their father—it just wrote itself in some ways. That's how series work: you define the characters, and then the stories emerge."

Each film in *The Christies* was built around a limited visual language, which Mulloy deliberately simplified. As Mulloy explained,

> There are about five images of a face-on view, five in profile. Each character had maybe 10 images, and there were around eight characters. So maybe 80 images total. I kept changing it—I'd tell people, 'Oh, I have this many,' but I never really counted. Didn't see the point.

This stripped-back approach to animation allowed him to focus on the characters' voices and the absurdity of their situations rather than relying on elaborate visuals.

As with all of his work, Mulloy defiantly chose to create images that went against the Hollywood norm:

> Why, working as an individual, would I want to recreate the clichés of the dominant industrial cinema? My method of creating is to do with speed and the creation of what Hollywood fans would generally consider to be ugly. In *The Christies*, for instance, each character has only about ten different frames of drawings for their face. To draw these faces, I used a digital brush that was so big, it was impossible for me to control. All ten drawings took about ten minutes. The same thing for the backgrounds. The images were the first things that came into my head.

*The Christies'* animation style, with its flat, simplistic figures, lends itself well to the often uncomfortable, dark humor of the series. The lack of complex backgrounds or movements creates a kind of surreal, disorienting space where the focus is entirely on the dialogue and the characters' absurd, often vicious behavior. Mulloy would often incorporate strange, minimalist backgrounds—like the occasional circular blobs or maps—to keep the attention on the interactions between the family members. This visual minimalism forces the viewer to engage more deeply with the dialogue, which is the heart of Mulloy's critique.

Each film in the trilogy took about a year to complete and was entirely unscripted. Mulloy explained that the process was improvisational, noting,

> It was made on the fly in the order it was finally shown in. I began each episode of the trilogy pretty much not knowing anything about where I was going, and that is how I continued. Every few days I would complete a scene and then move on. This is how the films grew, one scene after another.

There was little revision along the way, with Mulloy admitting, "I cannot remember rewriting any dialogue, or redrawing any of the images." Despite working alone on the films, he decided to add a touch of Hollywood-style flair to the credits, saying,

> Although it was only me that worked on the film, I decided to put full-length credits on the end. I made these up and put them on each film in the trilogy. I figured that people would take the film more seriously if they thought a lot of people had worked on it, and it had cost more money.

He knew some people might get all hot and bothered thinking a lot of money had been wasted on such a bizarre and minimalist work, but naturally he was unbothered: "I was okay with that too."

*The Christies*' world functions like a distorted mirror of reality, where Mulloy critiques the various social and cultural structures we accept as

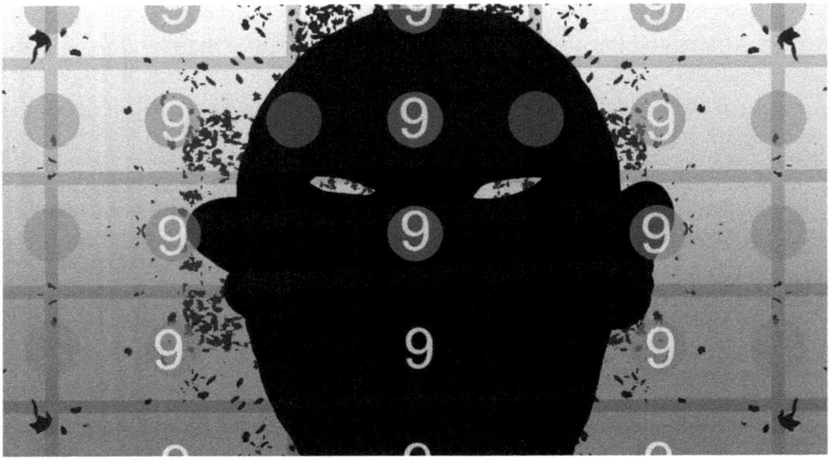


Ms Okobe

normal. The simplicity of the animation and the starkness of the characters allow Mulloy to cut through the complexities of modern life, creating an environment where everything is laid bare—without adornment or pretense. The characters may be exaggerated, but their flaws, desires, and hypocrisies are painfully real, reflecting the contradictions that lie within us all.

## NOTES

1 From the film, *Trust* (1990) written and directed by Hal Hartley.
2 Chris Robinson, *Unsung Heroes of Animation* (Bloomington, IN: John Libbey Publishing, 2005), p. 106.
3 https://liaf.org.uk/phil-mulloy-interview

# Endgame

# 5

After *The Christies*, Mulloy didn't vanish from the festival circuit, but his presence certainly grew quieter as family life took precedence. While he never stopped making films, he mostly stopped submitting them to festivals. During this period, Mulloy continued to refine his craft, possibly more than ever. It was a time of both successes and misfires, but some noteworthy works did emerge, including *Endgame* and, more recently, the haunting and heartbreaking *Once Upon a Time on Earth*.

Mulloy recalls that during this quieter phase, his personal life had a significant impact on his creative output. "About eight years ago, my daughter got a divorce," he explains. "She came back from New York, really upset, and stayed with us, bringing her kids with her."

While Mulloy's family life took precedence, he was still involved in his work. "I was still doing things—I made that film about two guys going off for the weekend to fire guns," he says, referring to *Endgame*.

Though Mulloy's creative output slowed at least from a public perspective, he continued to work. "With the kids around, I just couldn't work up the

Birds of Paradise

DOI: 10.1201/9781003527909-5

enthusiasm to come into my room," he admits. "Spending time with the kids felt better than sitting alone in my room trying to work. But I was still doing some things."

***Birds of Paradise* (2013)** follows the direction Mulloy began exploring in *On the Coastline*. It's an unusual piece consisting of live-action footage of a group of students standing in front of a brick wall, occasionally gazing skyward. After some time, a digital naked man appears on screen, performing modern dance, twisting his body into impossible shapes and sometimes even disassembling himself. It becomes, at times, tedious, then comical. Eventually, the man flies off, and the screen turns black. "I shot something at a festival in Italy—it was some kind of horror festival. I took photos of these kids looking up at something in the sky. At the time, I didn't know what I'd use it for, but I thought I'd put this together with something at some point."

Mulloy would use a similar technique in the unreleased experiment *Bathroom Blues* (2015) and the *Sleepwalke*r series (2013–14), which consists of around 14 films, all featuring a similar-looking digital character first seen in *Birds of Paradise*.

In *Bathroom Blues*, the digital character simply sits on a toilet while a man showers in the background. I imagined it as an ode to constipation, but Mulloy admits, "I don't really know what it was about. I was just using some random shots I'd taken in Brazil."

In *Sleepwalker*, the digital character roams through various urban exteriors and interiors. "There was this software called Poser," Mulloy says.

> It looked like something for teenagers, like 16- or 17-year-olds, where they could undress dolls. The men had penises, the women had vaginas. But

Sleepwalker

> what interested me was that if you manipulated the figures incorrectly, they couldn't move properly. They just broke apart into weird shapes, and I thought, 'That's interesting—I can use that.'

*Sleepwalker* originated during a trip to Kansas, where Mulloy was invited to give a talk at a local college.

> Before I left, I bought a camera at the airport. I shot an image of a hotel—don't know if you've seen that one. It's just a hotel. And while I was there, I could hear these long trains passing. They go on for miles across America. Since I had that figure from Poser, I placed it in front of the shot—just in the hotel corridor. Not the lobby, but a crummy hotel corridor. And it worked. I liked that figure, just walking with his eyes closed.

*Sleepwalker* is a strange and eerie series, filled with a sense of oppressive silence and distance. It accidentally becomes a reflection of an abandoned world—something that evokes the feeling of the pandemic experience a few years later.

As with all of his work, Mulloy found great pleasure in experimenting:

> I just decided—I've got this camera, wherever I go, I'll take pictures. I'd walk around, throw the camera up, turn it, try different angles, then place the figure in front of it. Then I added sounds. I wanted to experiment with sound. We were in New York because my daughter, Lucy, was living there at the time. When her child was born, we visited a lot. I shot something in the snow on the Lower East Side of Manhattan. I just enjoyed making images—without people in them. The idea was to capture a space, then use the character to dramatize it. Then I'd go back over the space again. It was abstract—nothing specific. That fascinated me. For example, I was in a church, and I did it there. This naked figure walking around the church… Anyway, it was just something on the side.

These side projects showcase Mulloy's playfulness and unending creative curiosity.

> That was when I became interested in figuring out how to make animation with as little effort as possible. So I was always looking for things—finding pieces to use, putting them together. I just keep searching. I imagine a lot of animators work that way, constantly figuring out what to do next. I used to laugh at them for that, thinking, 'I just do cowboys.'

In 2015, Mulloy made ***Endgame***—about two guys whose planned weekend fun of war games goes horrifically wrong—his most successful film since *The Christies*. It marked a return to his dark comic voice and somewhat recognizable visual style, except this time his characters were seen from a distance and appeared like ants. He made a few films using this 'ant' style, including *Metaphor* (2015), *Deadman's Dream* (2015), and *2019* (2019).

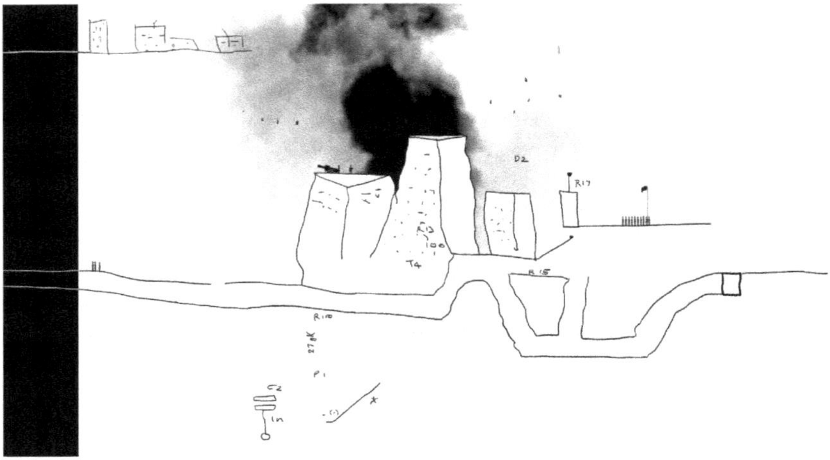

*Endgame*

Mulloy recalled:

> I became interested in how people look like little flies from afar and thought that looking at things from a distance was fascinating. I got obsessed with the idea—though I don't think I fully achieved it—that you can show people from a distance, without knowing who they are, what they're doing, or how they relate to each other. Just silhouettes. You see them shake hands, sit down, one runs off, another arrives—it creates an exchange, but you don't really know what's happening. The audience has to figure it out. That was my goal. But in the end, I made things like *Endgame*, where you can see what's going on—just two nerds thinking they're tough guys.

The brilliance of *Endgame* lies in its ant-sized characters. Without that scale—along with Mulloy's superb pacing—the film wouldn't have worked as well, especially in scenes like having a tree shoved up someone's backside. Like Mulloy's finest work, we laugh at truly horrible things, but we also become implicated not just by our laughter but perhaps by how accustomed we've become to seeing violence.

"I became fascinated with using faceless characters who go through terrible things," Mulloy adds.

> You don't see their reactions, but at some point, you still identify with them. It's like *Sex Life of a Chair*—it becomes something in your head. That's the power of suggestion. What's in your mind can be worse than what's actually shown. If you don't show it explicitly, the audience experiences it in their own heads.

Mulloy was initially inspired by a Serbian man he knew in Wales.

> He'd go off to fight in the Balkans for two weeks, then come back like it was a normal thing. They were firing rockets. He'd go over there, fight, then return to his regular life. People actually do that. Originally, I was thinking about paintball—how people want the thrill of being kids again, playing soldier, and getting a kick out of it.

Throughout his work, Mulloy has frequently explored our complicated relationship with violence and war. We're horrified by it, but at the same time, we're drawn to it. "There's an attraction, even though it's repulsive," Mulloy adds. "It's like how newspapers would show images of people in concentration camps—Jewish prisoners waiting to be liberated by the Americans or Russians—right next to photos of half-naked women. There's a strange, unsettling juxtaposition."

Having grown up in the aftermath of World War II, Mulloy was often exposed to its horrors, but, beyond that, he has always had a somewhat schizoid relationship with violence.

> I remember reading a book—I forget the title now—about Christian martyrs in ancient Rome, saints being executed in the amphitheaters. It disgusted me, but I was fascinated by it. I would seek it out even though it made me feel sick. I think those early feelings have always been present in my films—this shock at what humanity is capable of.

*2019*

***2019*** was made in a similar vein to *Endgame,* but this time the focus is on a man, a woman, and some intrusive ants. The man and woman kiss, then part ways. The man sits on a bridge for a while before walking past a car and an office tower. Suddenly, an ant appears with a giant chair. The man returns to his car and drives. Eventually, we see a man atop a giant chair. A small audience waits below, and he is impatiently waiting for someone's arrival. A car appears. The man exits and climbs a ladder to the top of the chair. The first man seems to start tap dancing. The second man leaves, gets a gun, and is about to shoot the tap dancer but hesitates. Piles of ants appear, disrupting the scene. It's as if the ants are the directors of this "play." It becomes increasingly difficult to distinguish the characters from one another, and maybe that's the point.

The story seems to lose focus a bit, with more scenes involving the ladder, the gun, the man and woman, the ants, and people jumping off a cliff. In the end, the man seems to be devoured by the ants. Is this some anti-human play imagined by an artistic ant community? Probably not, but I like imagining that's true.

Mulloy was not satisfied with *2019.*

> It just doesn't add up to anything in the end. I spent a long time wondering, 'Is this going to turn into a love story?' It begins with a woman running off, a man chasing her. They argue. You don't need any dialogue—it's just these two little creatures interacting. She runs off, he follows in a car, she hides… I kept thinking, 'Where do I take this?' Eventually, I had the idea of the chair. But it never added up. I was trying to salvage it as I went, hoping it would evolve into something. But it never quite did.

"It's like—I never really found what I was looking for. My heart just wasn't in it. You know what I mean? Sometimes stories write themselves and you're in the flow. But some ideas, no matter how much you try, just don't go anywhere. This one felt like that."

Initially, I interpreted this as another of Mulloy's satires on people in power, but he claims it was really "just this guy showing off, being better than the other guy." "Maybe that's what it lacked—an actual point," Mulloy continues.

> Back then, especially during the first Trump era, real life became more surreal than anything you could dream up. I think I felt like, if I made a political film, it would just be repeating what I did back in the '90s. So instead, I tried to make something more surreal—just about life, people interacting. But like I said, my heart wasn't in it. I didn't quite know where I was going.

***In the Future (2019)*** has rough elements reminiscent of *Endgame,* but the characters are larger in size. It gives off the vibe of a kid scribbling away on paper. Someone says, "I love you," a man whistles and pees. The man wanders underwater, where he thinks we will all live. Another man arrives and tells him to stop whistling. The voices are computer-generated, slightly different from the ones used in *The Christies* series. It feels like a story created by an ADD child, but as an adult. Chairs talk, as do strange animal/human hybrids. There is a talk about drifting toward barbarism. One character speaks of

In the Future

Happily Ever After

a thoughtless society that wouldn't even offer him a seat on a bus because people are too busy staring at their phones.

"The guy whistling and peeing—that was the starting point," says Mulloy.

> I found this sound clip of someone whistling. It was such a nothing whistle—tuneless, like someone whose brain's just idling. So I imagined this guy walking, stopping, peeing. That's it. The film itself—it was just a sequence of moments that popped into my head. But the main idea was: Where are we headed? What's the future bringing? And at the time, things didn't feel very hopeful. Still don't, really.
>
> So I ended it with this crash—a bad note, literally. Like a piece of terrible music to finish on. By that point, it just felt more obvious to everyone—Trump had already been in power, then there were the Capitol riots.

***Happily Ever After* (2022)** was one of the few films from this period to be submitted to festivals. Mulloy returns to the world of *2019*, but with more structure and success. A red curtain appears and opens to reveal a sketchy, *Endgame*-like world. A woman leaves home and walks off-screen. The ants appear and remove the sets, as would happen in live theater. The story centers on a man and a woman who are fated to be together, but obstacles keep getting in the way. When they finally do hook up, the man gets distracted by fame and fortune. The woman ends up destroying his world, literally reducing him to a man-child. From there, a battle rages between the man and woman, seemingly over control (sounds like most marriages). All of this takes place in the world of the ants, who are the ones putting on this human play. In the end, the couple finds a sort of compromise: they are together, though not looking at each other, feeding the ants. That seems to be the best they can hope for in this chaotic existence.

"I liked the idea of small creatures being the ones in control," adds Mulloy.

> They move the scenery, they determine the setting—it's symbolic. The ants are fate, or destiny. They're the ones putting the pieces in place, moving the characters around. And in *Happily Ever After*, the relationship breaks down because of the man's behavior, but also because of what the ants are doing behind the scenes. Eventually, the woman takes charge—but then a threat shows up, and she needs him. So it becomes about this uneasy balance—feeding the system that's controlling them in order to keep going.

*Happily Ever After*, like much of Mulloy's work, brings to mind shadow puppets or silhouettes. Mulloy has never worked directly with shadow puppets, but he loves the simplicity of shadows.

> Just light and movement. It's a very simple means of creating a kind of intense effect. I think that's what I've always gone for. I don't like being too literal. I like suggestion. It's more about the rhythm, the composition, the way things feel, than spelling everything out.

The influence of shadow puppets also connects to the primal nature of Mulloy's work. His characters are barely even people—more like ideas or instincts. "Yes, they're often more symbolic than anything else. Stripped down. I'm not interested in realism—at least not in the conventional sense. I think if you go too realistic, it kills the mystery."

This search for the stripped-down and the abstract has followed Mulloy throughout his animation career, and he says it even extends to his earlier work. "Even when I started with live action, I was never really chasing a polished look. I wanted things to feel raw. I still do. It's just how I process the world."

Mulloy says that simplicity is important to him because

> it's the closest thing to magic. I like taking things that aren't much—things you might throw away—and turning them into something bigger. That idea comes from art. Artists transform what others discard. Like Picasso taking a bicycle seat and turning it into a bull's head. That kind of thing. But also, there's a kind of magic in simplicity itself. It's not about hiding things behind lots of technique. You can see how it's made, everything's there—but somehow it still sparks something in your mind. That's the kind of animation I like. Where you're not overloaded. You're given space to think, to feel something beyond what's on the screen.

It's an approach that is rare in animation, and to find similar examples in cinema, one might point to Aki Kaurismäki or one of Mulloy's influences, Robert Bresson.

> His films are just made up of shots. Simple. Constructed in blocks. You feel that structure, but the tension's still there. Unlike a Hollywood film, where the whole idea is to hide how it's built. With Bresson, the construction is part of it, and yet it still carries deep emotion. It's democratic, in a way. It allows the viewer to participate. It doesn't force-feed. It gives you space to complete the film in your head.

Unfortunately, most audiences seem to want mindless spectacle. Mulloy doesn't do mindless or spectacle.

## *THE LETTER A*, 2022

Another unreleased film, *The Letter A*, combines elements of *The Christies* and *Endgame* but with a distinct bleakness. It feels different from anything else Mulloy has done.

A child recalls a dream about seeing a gigantic letter "A." With a jetpack, he flies up near the top of the letter. Eyes suddenly appear on the letter, and it begins to walk away. The boy then encounters a UFO, enters it, and flies off. A man's voice harshly replaces the boy's voice. The UFO crashes, and the boy survives, walking toward a letter "A."

In the second part, a woman's voice appears, followed by the harsh voice of the man returning. Birds sit in a tree, with barking dogs nearby. The boy recalls how his dad told him the world is filled with magical things. The computer-simulated voices, which bring to mind *The Christies*, all seem to be the voices of the boy. It's a baffling film that truly resembles the ambiguity of a dream, with a strange sadness throughout—one that anticipates the bleakness of *Once Upon A Time on Earth*, with no black humor to relieve us.

The Letter A

> It started when I was having coffee. I go for walks a lot, and there's a park café I used to visit with the kids. We'd sit outside and watch jackdaws steal bread. It started with the jackdaws. I don't know where it was going. I just started with 'A' and kept going. Those films come from a different place. A bit arty-farty, really. They were never meant for festivals. It was me saying, 'Screw it—just make the films you want to make.'

With that same mindset comes ***The Man in the Spoon*** (2022), another unreleased experiment. A man (voiced by Mulloy) momentarily recounts a childhood home long gone. You'd be hard-pressed to even recognize this as a Mulloy film, as he uses a mix of chalk and assorted objects to create a unique visual style. It's a mysterious and haunting work set in a seaside village, where the atmosphere is thick with an eerie sense of loss.

At one point, a fisherman kills a fish, and elsewhere, at the bottom of the water, a small spoon appears, reflecting a face. A storm soon devours the ship, and a mysterious insect emerges, possessing a goddess-like aura. As the storm rages, the bodies of the men lie at the bottom of the sea, their fate sealed. Throughout, a steady, haunting keyboard soundtrack plays, contributing to the sense of something ending. The film's composition feels like a meditation on loss and the passage of time, with its cryptic imagery and melancholy tone.

Here, we see Mulloy in full experimental mode. To achieve the chalk look, he used

> bits of paper. I rubbed the paper so it got this texture—it would rip a bit, look rough. I was moving away from digital, from Wacom. Trying to make it look handmade, raw. There's a bit with a big fish. I used a little torch,

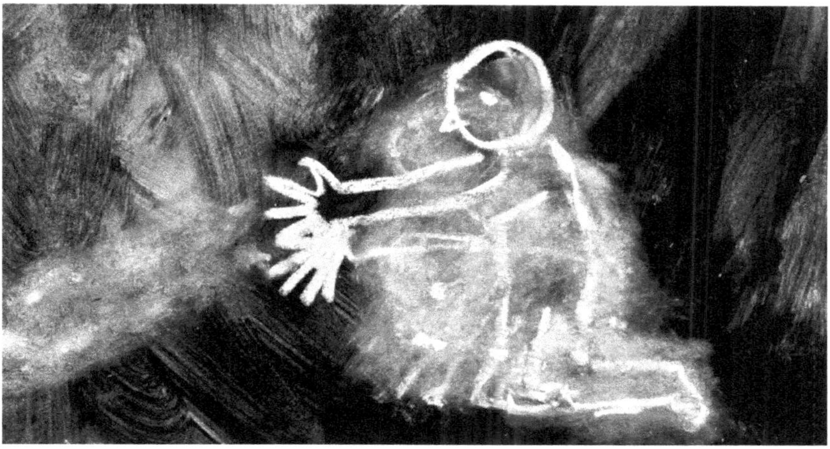

The Man in the Spoon

> flicking the light as I filmed. It gave the body this weird three-dimensional feel. Just playing with effects. Interesting, but again—doesn't make a film.

*The Man in the Spoon* was inspired by a pile of spoons Mulloy found in a secondhand shop. "I went into a junk shop and they had a whole lot of spoons, so I bought a pile of them," he recalls.

> I was thinking—people collect these things, what do they represent? What do they mean to them? Some of them have castles on them. I thought they're really boring things. Really quite boring. People buy them, so I thought, 'I'll do something with these—these are boring enough for me.'

That impulse—to find something expressive in the discarded and mundane—drives the film's strange tone. "I always think of them as very British," Mulloy adds.

> And there's something of that I wanted. There's one image in it, towards the end, that looks like a Black guy—or came from that kind of iconography—and that comes up at the end. This kind of Britishness... I thought I'd just create something out of these spoons, these bits and pieces on the ends—like castles, or swans. That was the main thinking.

Despite the intriguing premise and the haunting tone of the finished piece, Mulloy remained ambivalent about the results. "It's not got the kind of vigor of something... and in the end, you think. Oh, okay, so what? So I never shared that."

It's another example of a Mulloy work that resists easy classification—a film assembled from fragments, steeped in atmosphere, and haunted by a quiet sense of futility.

Mulloy's most recent work is ***Once Upon a Time on Earth* (2024)**. In a post-apocalyptic suburb of London, a man prepares for a perilous journey by pumping air into his bike tires—then inflating his son's cherished green balloon. Together with his wife, they set off across a bleak, ravaged landscape, encountering drones, alligators, torrential downpours, and rising floods. When tragedy strikes, the son is left to continue alone, facing an equally uncertain future.

While the film retains Mulloy's signature minimalist design and biting social commentary, the usual sardonic humor is notably absent—and for good reason. The state of the world offers little to chuckle about. Echoing *The Road* by Cormac McCarthy, O*nce Upon a Time on Earth* is a devastating, poignant, yet cautiously hopeful speculation on the future that may await us… if we don't get our shit together.

And it all started with a bicycle.

"I didn't know what I was doing, except I drew a picture of a bicycle," admits Mulloy.

> I was thinking of Michael Dudok de Wit—maybe because of his film *Father and Daughter.* I wanted to move things without having them walk—a bicycle is great for that. All you need is the legs going round. So it began like that, and I drew different-sized bicycles. I was still interested in very small bicycles, very small people, little silhouettes going along the horizon.

After realizing that he couldn't sustain this concept for long, he started developing bigger characters.

Once Upon a Time on Earth

> I realized I wasn't going to keep them consistent. The boy's size shifts—sometimes he's bigger, more manly, sometimes a baby. It was like what I did in *Happily Ever After*. You can change the size of the character to reflect how they're feeling. You can control that a little bit. And I just began a sort of journey. I've been using explosions quite a bit. You don't have to animate them fully; they're kind of free. I used them in *Endgame*. Most people try to make them look like real explosions. I just did them in black and white. It felt more like splashing ink or flicking ink onto stuff. So yeah, I started with smoke going up—the journey begins.

Mulloy had no idea where he was going from there—except that he had the idea to have people trying to escape from England, a concept that eerily echoes the deportations taking place in the USA in 2025.

"So they start off, and there's this rain sequence," Mulloy recalls. "I used very simple means. I was filming skies—some dramatic, some plain—and I thought, 'I'll use these.' They gave me a steady horizon line. I kept things simple, reused the same elements in slightly different ways. There's something satisfying about that—like cataloguing different kinds of movement. It's a bit like music—you start with a theme and play it in slightly different ways. I like that. I like simple music—church music, drone music—the repetition with slight differences. It creates cohesiveness."

"I used these landscapes, then thought about how to change them, make them more interesting—so I introduced water, rain effects. I was able to find these elements—thunder, lightning, rain—online. Like, I'd use a flashlight, flash it on black paper for lightning. And I used those in scenes. You're using someone else's work, in a way, but it was perfect."

While this apocalyptic setting could be almost anywhere, Mulloy purposely set it in England.

> In the beginning, the film was more about a state—like Russia—they were escaping under surveillance. But I got rid of all that. No need to show it. People already understand what it means to flee something bad. I had to redo the whole beginning to get rid of the drones and things. These are English people emigrating. This is what happens. It's been happening since Iraq—when the Americans went in And Libya, when they got rid of Gaddafi. They're traveling through this Britain that's unfamiliar. The land has changed—you don't recognize it. It's not a London suburb. You go out into a river and rain—it's maybe too strong to say 'alien,' but it's unfamiliar.

As bleak as *Once Upon a Time on Earth* is, there is a flicker of hope in the form of the green balloon—an idea Mulloy had from the start, though not originally thinking of it as a symbol of optimism.

> At first, it was just the father blowing something up and giving it to the child. But as they move, the balloon moves backwards—it creates a sense

> of motion. And also, you get sound. The noise I use at the end? That's the balloons banging together. It's not drumming—it's just balloons. It just happened. I didn't plan it. I just hoped something like that would come together. You get a close-up of the coach or cart, and you hear the banging. That became the ending. That noise. A kind of protest, in a way.

-

Mulloy's recent films, even if not fully satisfying to him, remain compelling. These works, though often unfinished or unrefined in his eyes, reveal an artist unafraid to confront his own imperfections. They reflect a commitment to his craft that extends beyond seeking approval or validation. "I just have high standards for what I think is worth putting out there," he admits. Yet, even when his work doesn't hit the mark, it still undeniably carries his distinct voice. It's evident that for Mulloy, the process is just as important as the product. "I can't not do it," he says of his continual output, whether it's drawing, writing, or animating. "That's the one constant. Even if I'm not showing them, I'm still doing it. It's how I think."

This kind of honesty is rare in film-making. Many creators shy away from acknowledging their failures, but Mulloy embraces them as part of the artistic process. "I think it's important," he reflects. "Otherwise, you just keep recycling the same stuff, pretending it all means something when maybe it doesn't. And sometimes it doesn't. Sometimes the idea doesn't land, or you lose your way, or your heart's just not in it."

This constant search for new ways to express the inexpressible, even when the results are messy or unresolved, is what keeps his work alive. This constant cycle of experimentation, failure, and self-reflection is what defines his work. It's unpredictable, sometimes messy, and often unresolved—but always genuine.

# Raw Outrage

# 6

There's something deeply human about the way Phil Mulloy talks about his work. Not in the sentimental sense. Not romanticized. More like: flawed, raw, maybe even a little scrappy. But alive. And that aliveness—that *movement*—is the point.

He talks about his early set-ups with a kind of amused disbelief. Steenbecks in the barn, 16mm tape recorders being thrown out and salvaged. "Everything was improvised as I went along," he tells me. "Technological changes helped. Things got cheaper. In the early days of computers, trying to get things to work was hard. I started with Steenbecks—editing by hand, trying to put the sound on."

You can imagine him out in Wales, in that barn, fumbling through trial-and-error, not waiting for permission, just doing what he could with what he had. There's a kind of purity in that—not naive, just focused. Clear-eyed.

And it's that clarity—of purpose, not outcome—that seems to drive him. "I still spend 8 to 10 hours a day in my room working," he says. "It's the pleasure of doing—not even showing the films—just doing. Seeing where it takes you." That phrase stuck with me. *Just doing.* It sounds simple. It isn't.

He talks a lot about that early influence from American underground cinema. People who developed their own film made things outside the system. "That idea of carrying on stayed with me." It's not about legacy or recognition. It's about being inside the work, day after day, letting it unfold.

And yet, even after decades of making, he doubts. He catches himself repeating patterns. "I can see the last films are getting a bit lumpen," he admits. "I should be working quicker, doing things differently." There's no resting on instincts. He's constantly second-guessing, course-correcting, trying to stay light on his feet. "The computer is seductive," he says. "You want to see what it looks like. But then you lose the impulse to shove it along, to go wild."

Mulloy's almost always been his own producer, crew, and audience. It's a lonely but fiercely independent space. "It's just me," he shrugs. "I want to make something. I want to say something. But I also want it to be simple. I never know where it's going. Sometimes you go down the wrong street and have to walk back. But then you put the sound on, and it comes alive."

DOI: 10.1201/9781003527909-6

This Isn't Me

Even as he shifted styles—cowboys, commandments, Zogs—he often kept the same black-and-white visual rhythm. Not out of stubbornness, but because it freed him up. "It was like handwriting," he says. "I didn't need to think. I could just turn it out."

But eventually, he knew he needed to change. *The Christies* were a turning point: color, new textures, looser rules. "I thought, I've kind of milked this cow," he says, deadpan. It's a classic Mulloy line—dry, self-aware, a little dismissive, but with real clarity underneath. He'd pushed one approach as far as it could go. Now it was time to move on.

So he made things even simpler. "I thought, go the whole hog—give them nothing. Let the audience do the work." He found constraint opened doors. "You can make humor if you set very tight parameters," he says. "You come up with solutions I find fascinating."

But digital tools come with their own challenges. "Everything's smooth now. I like things that flicker and jump. I find them more alive."

There's something almost punk about his resistance to polish. Not in style necessarily, but in spirit. He resists gloss. Resists ease. Resists anything that makes the work too clean, too safe, too predictable.

And he's deeply uninterested in the machinery of the industry. "These days, it all comes out of graphics. I come from painting—experimenting, trying things out. It was looser." The idea of a packaged script, pitched and polished? "I think that's kind of foolish."

Money has never been the motivator. "Maybe I'm an idealist," he says. "I try to keep my work free from money—filthy lucre. I'm more interested in earning money in other ways, separate from my work." Even back when arts funding was more generous, he often sidestepped it. "I didn't get any money for *Ten Commandments*. I just made them."

There's a stubborn freedom in that. It means making the film is the reward. The process is the point. "If you want that kind of freedom—where you don't need a script, where you can just go somewhere and see where it takes you—you have to work differently."

And that's what he's always done. Worked differently.

Still, there's a limit to what satire can do when the real world becomes its own grotesque cartoon. "It's like a satire of itself," he says. "But it's a satire that's also a threat, which makes it pretty scary." His work's gotten bleaker. More stripped down. Less pointed commentary, more existential dread. "I've always been bleak," he says, almost proudly.

But it's not cruelty. It's critique. "Everything I've done, even if it's aggressive, comes from a place of calling out how things are organized. It's not against people. I'm not interested in putting down the little man."

And maybe that's the thread. Across all the films, from the raw ink-splattered early shorts to the darkly formal Zog sagas—Mulloy's trying to strip things back. To scratch off the surface and look at what's underneath. What systems shape us? What habits do we repeat? What rules don't we even realize we're following?

It's clear, though, that the shift to digital tools has changed the tone of his work. Phil's not blind to the advantages that technology brings—sophistication, smoother results, more control—but he's always resisted the sheen that comes with perfection. "Everything in digital cinema is smooth now," he says, with a note of frustration. "I try to prick that bubble of slickness. To show what's underneath." For Mulloy, the simplicity, the rawness, the flicker of imperfection—it's where the pulse of the work lives. He doesn't want the polished surface that digital can deliver. He wants something with a little more life, something with edges, something you can feel.

It's a statement on the nature of art, and maybe on the world itself. There's something inauthentic about the constant push for smoothness. For perfection. Mulloy doesn't have time for it. Not when there's something raw, something underneath that needs to come out. In times like these, that underneath—whether it's in the work or in the world—deserves to be seen.

Once Upon a Time on Earth

# Bibliography


Kitson, Clare. *British Animation: The Channel 4 Factor*. Bloomington: Indiana University Press, 2008.

McSorley Tom & Chris Robinson (eds). *The Corners are Glowing: Selected Writings from the Ottawa International Animation Festival*. Boca Raton: CRC Press, 2023.

Robinson, Chris. *Unsung Heroes of Animation*. London: John Libbey Publishing, 2005.

Wiedemann, Julius (ed). *Animation Now!* Los Angeles, CA: Taschen America Llc, 2004.

# Selected Filmography

*Allow Me, 1970*
*Eye of the Storm, 1989*
*Tinfish, 1990*
*Cowboys: High Noon, 1991*
*Cowboys: Murder, 1991*
*Cowboys: Outrage, 1991*
*Cowboys: Slim Pickin's, 1991*
*Cowboys: That's Nothin', 1991*
*Cowboys: The Conformist, 1991*
*Possession, 1991*
*Ding Dong, 1992*
*The Sound of Music, 1993*
*Laughing Moon Films, 1993/1994*
*The History of the World: The Age of Reason Begins, 1993*
*The History of the World: The Discovery of Language, 1994*
*The History of the World: The Invention of Writing and Its Destruction*
*Great Moments in Film, 1995*
*The Ten Commandments:*
*No. 1 Thou Shalt Not Adore False Gods, 1995*
*No. 2 Thou Shalt Not Commit Blasphemy, 1995*
*No. 3 Remember to Keep Holy The Sabbath, 1995*
*No. 4 Honour Thy Father and Thy Mother, 1995*
*No. 5 Thou Shalt Not Kill, 1994*
*No. 6 Thou Shalt Not Commit Adultery, 1994*
*No. 7 Thou Shalt Not Steal, 1994*
*No. 8 Thou Shalt Not Bear False Witness, 1995*
*No. 9 Thou Shalt Not Covet Thy Neighbour's Goods, 1996*
*No. 10 Thou Shalt Not Covet Thy Neighbour's Wife, 1996*
*The Wind of Changes, 1996*
*The Chain, 1997*
*The Sexlife of a Chair, 1998*
*Season's Greetings, 1999*
*Intolerance, 2000*
*Flik Flak, 2001*
*Intolerance II: The Invasion 2001*
*The Henries, 2001*
*Love is Strange, 2002*
*Intolerance III: The Final Solution 2003*
*The Christies, 2006*
*On the Coastline, 2006*

*Brockwell Park, 2007*
*Goodbye Mister Christie, 2008*
*Dead But Not Buried, 2010*
*The Christies Spots for Holland Animation Film Festival, 2010*
*The Pain and the Pity, 2013*
*Christie series for Channel 4, 2013:*
*Little Terry's Dream*
*Sex on Tv*
*The Sex Slave of Tunbridge Wells*
*Strawberry Cheesecake*
*Terry's Departure*
*The Banker*
*Backwards Forwards*
*Bird of Paradise, 2013*
*Manipulation, 2013*
*Sleepwalker, 2015*
*Endgame, 2015*
*The, 2015*
*That Sound, 2015*
*These Guys are Unbelievable, 2015*
*One Minute Trilogy, 2015*
*The Deadman's Dream, 2015*
*Preparing to Fly, 2015*
*Now I Think I'm Happy, 2018*
*Did You Have Sex with Boris, 2019*
*In the Future, 2019*
*2019, 2019*
*Happily Ever After, 2022*
*The Letter A, 2022*
*The Man in the Spoon, 2022*
*Once Upon A Time on Earth, 2024*

# Index

For Product Safety Concerns and Information please contact our EU representative GPSR@taylorandfrancis.com
Taylor & Francis Verlag GmbH, Kaufingerstraße 24, 80331 München, Germany

www.ingramcontent.com/pod-product-compliance
Ingram Content Group UK Ltd.
Pitfield, Milton Keynes, MK11 3LW, UK
UKHW021620271125
465482UK00005B/24
*9781032862118*